ENCOUNTERS WITH CHRIST

Encounters with Christ

Meditations on
Six Readings from the Gospel

Carlo Maria Martini, SJ
Cahal Brendan Daly
Adrianus J Simonis
Jean-Marie Lustiger
Godfried Danneels
George Basil Hume, OSB

Hodder & Stoughton
LONDON SYDNEY AUCKLAND

Contents

Introduction

The Centenary of the laying of the foundation stone of Westminster Cathedral in 1895 has provided the Cathedral with a wonderful opportunity to reflect on and deepen its own mission. An essential aspect of the Centenary has been to look at the foundation which must undergird every human life, namely spirituality.

In special evening services held each week throughout Lent in 1995, Cardinals from neighbouring countries in Europe were invited to give a meditation on a Gospel passage. The Cardinals gave half-hour meditations preceded by a proclamation of the Gospel and followed by silent prayer. In their mediations the Cardinals were asked to reflect on the relevance of the Gospel passage chosen as an encounter between Jesus and our society.

These encounters described in the Gospels, though rooted in time and space, nonetheless have a timeless quality about them. This is why the Gospel is relevant in every age. Each person with whom Jesus spoke represents us.

Cardinals, like Bishops, are called so often to deal with specific issues that confront society and the Church. It has been a joy and a privilege to listen to others, and to be able to speak about what lies deepest and is most urgent in every human life: personal contact with God.

I am very grateful to Eric Major and the editorial team at Hodder and Stoughton for their work in compiling these Lenten meditations into a book, so making them available to a wider audience.

Cardinal Basil Hume
Archbishop of Westminster
July 1995

Cardinal Carlo Maria Martini, SJ

Archbishop of Milan

Carlo Maria Martini was born in 1927 in Turin. After classical studies in the College of the Jesuit Fathers, he entered the Society of Jesus in 1944. After completing his studies in philosophy and theology, he was ordained priest in 1952.

From 1962 he held the chair of textual criticism in the Pontifical Biblical Institute in Rome and in 1964 he edited a new edition of the *Novum Testamentum Graece et Latine* by A. Merk and subsequently became a member of the committee for the publication of *The Greek New Testament*. In numerous studies he has tackled various aspects of the witness of the early Christian community as recorded in the New Testament.

From 1969 to 1978 he was Rector of the Pontifical Biblical Institute. The second edition of *The Greek New Testament* came out in 1975 and is the basis for over 800 versions of the Gospels currently available worldwide; Fr Martini was one of the five editors, and the only Catholic. In 1978 Pope Paul VI appointed him Rector Magnificus of the Gregorian University. During these years he published numerous books and articles of textual criticism and exegesis. In Italy and abroad he has devoted himself tirelessly to the field of apostolic activity and spiritual instruction. His ecumenical concern has led him to meet with Christians of other denominations. In 1979 Pope John Paul raised him to the Episcopal See of Milan and he was consecrated in St Peter's in 1980. The Pope created him Cardinal at the consistory of 2 February 1983, with the title of Santa Cecilia, and in the same year asked him to be Relator at the Synod of Bishops.

Cardinal Carlo Maria Martini, SJ
Archbishop of Milan

Jesus meets the rich young man:
confronting a materialistic society

(Mark 10:17–31)

1

When I was asked to take as my theme, 'Jesus meets the Rich Young Man: confronting a materialistic society', I felt it would need the qualities described at the beginning of Psalm 45 – a tongue as nimble as a writer's pen. Unfortunately, I find myself in the position of John Henry Newman when, in 1879, he wrote to the Pope to give the reasons why he considered himself unsuitable to be made a cardinal.

He felt that, among other things, his ignorance of foreign languages was a considerable obstacle to the nomination. I should add that the fact that I *am* a cardinal does not change my poor knowledge of English, so I understand Newman's feelings.

First of all, I asked myself about the meaning of the title. What lies behind it? Why was the topic chosen? The first part of the title refers to a Gospel passage, from St Mark 10:17–22, and parallel passages, and requires a scriptural explanation. But the second part of the title speaks of a 'materialistic' society and is implicitly identified with our society. It suggests that the words of Jesus to the rich young man have to mean something, not only for a single person, but for an entire community.

This leads to the question: are the words of Jesus to the rich young man still relevant for today? Do they sound too distant, unnatural, too dated? How are they to be translated for our time? And are the young people of today, in particular, and people generally still able to put relevant questions to Jesus and to wait for some answers?

3

With these and similar questions in mind I come to St Mark chapter 10 and I feel that to deal with the problem satisfactorily verses 17–32 should be considered with their division into three parts:

1 The Rich Man and Jesus (vv. 17–22).
2 Jesus and the Rich People – from the words, 'How hard it is for those who have riches to enter the kindom of God', to 'All things are possible with God.' (vv. 23–7).
3 Jesus and the Disciples – the answer to the words of Peter, 'We have left everything and followed you!' (vv. 28–31).

These three parts probably have different origins and came together here because they treat the same problems, of riches, and of earthly goods in relation to the kingdom of God. They belong also to a larger context, that of chapter 10 as a whole, which includes teachings about family life, marriage, divorce and children. The entire section should then be considered in order to understand the guidance of Jesus on these subjects. But here we have to limit ourselves to the short passage of the meeting of Jesus with the rich man, although we shall try to read it in the light of the context.

It is appropriate to mention here that this passage has often been addressed by the Holy Father, Pope John Paul II, especially in two documents. The first is the letter to the young people of all the world, written for the international year of youth in 1985. The second is the encyclical, 'Veritatis Splendor', of 1993, in which the Pope writes at length of morality and good moral behaviour in the light of the question posed by the rich young man and the answer of Jesus.

We come, then, to the text of the Gospel. The structure

of the narrative is very simple: a double question put to Jesus, a double answer and a final reaction of the so-called 'rich young man'.

Who really was this man? For Mark the answer is: someone without specific qualification. At the end of the passage we learn that 'he had great possessions'. He is said to have been 'a young man' in the parallel text of Matthew 19:20, and a 'magistrate', a 'ruler' in Luke 18:18. But behind the face of this man we can see the face of each one of us, whatever our ages or positions in society.

This man has a positive idea of Jesus. He calls him 'Good master'. Perhaps he has seen Jesus holding with love the little child of which Mark tells in the previous passage. In any case, he looks to Jesus as someone whom he can trust. Someone like that was rare and the young man was glad to have found one like Jesus. As a young man, he wanted to be confronted with an adult who had experience and wisdom and to whom he could speak without the fear of being misunderstood or of being considered a young dreamer.

He puts to Jesus the decisive question: 'What must I do to receive eternal life?' By these words he means that he wants to attain something of absolute value, something lasting, which does not disappoint.

The same question can be put in many other different ways, but in substance remains the same. How can I get something of lasting value, which will never deceive me?

The answer of Jesus emphasises two points. First, if you really trust someone for his goodness, you trust the source of all goodness, who is God. A true relationship with God has first to be secured in order to achieve something which is not disappointing. Second, that to get something of value you have to enter into a good relationship with other people, into the kind of relationship of fairness and justice so clearly expressed in the Ten Commandments.

Cardinal Basil Hume, in his report of the ten days'

meeting of the Bishop's Conference of England and Wales (September 1993), used these words of explanation, 'For the disciple the relationship with the Lord is the foundation of a sound personal moral life and a call to a style of life which reflects his priorities' (p. 4).

We can now ask: how far is this answer of Jesus understandable for today's world? And again: how can it be received by ordinary men and women, when many of our people in Europe do not belong any more to any organised form of religion and, while still believing in God as a mysterious force or spirit, do not believe in a personal God in the Christian sense? How can it be said effectively to them: God is good, he is the supreme value; keep his commandments and you will get the full realisation of your deepest desires and expectations?

It seems that we are facing in all our countries a profound crisis of religious identity which does not allow this first answer of Jesus to be received in its luminous clarity. But we have also to acknowledge – to use again the words of Cardinal Hume from the same document – that,

> Despite its evils, many features of our age demonstrate the innate dignity of the person and a real capacity for both compassion and contemplation . . . A profound respect for the dignity and autonomy of every individual is often afforded in our democratic society . . . individuals genuinely search for the 'good', both for themselves and for others . . . The majority of the people retain an instinct for the 'ultimate' or the transcendent.

That is to say that our society is not so intrinsically materialistic as it appears.

Thus we understand that the first question of the young man and the answer of Jesus are not alien to our time and our culture. If duly translated and correctly expressed, they are still relevant, they are meaningful and vital for our contemporaries.

But what about the following words of the Gospel, the exclamation of this man who says: 'I have obeyed all these commandments since my childhood'? In these words there is an affirmation of full loyalty to the law and a request for something more, a request which is made explicit in the Gospel of Matthew: 'What do I still lack?' (Matt. 19:20).

These words of full loyalty and obedience seem to belong to another era, to an atmosphere of conformity which is not of our times. In this context, I would say three things. First, this attitude was rare even in the time of Jesus: he wondered at these words and, as the Gospel says, 'looked steadily at him and loved him'. Such an affirmation of fidelity was not common. Even Peter had said to Jesus: 'Leave me Lord, for I am a sinful man!' (Luke 5:8).

Second, this loyalty is not so rare in our days as it may appear at first sight. Each one of us knows of many young people whose desires are very high, pure and intense. It is only necessary to have their trust and confidence – exactly the same as with Jesus and the young man.

Third, if we look not so much to what appears on the surface but to what lies within their hearts, we shall discover, to quote again the words of Cardinal Hume, that,

God's redeeming work is to be seen in so many aspects of the life of the people of our nations. Despite the pressures of a consumer-led, material-driven society, despite widespread hardship, there are many 'seeds of the word' to be found in our society . . . Throughout our society there are unmistakable signs of the redemptive presence of God, bringing about a deep longing for freedom, expressions of selfless love, noble generosity and courageous determination (p. 2).

We now come to the last words of Jesus: 'You lack one thing: go, sell what you have, and give to the poor, and you will have treasure in heaven; and come, follow me' (10:21). Five small revolutionary words: go, sell, give, come, follow! These words were a source of inspiration and conversion for innumerable people, from the first disciples to St Anthony, the Father of the monks in the desert, from St Francis of Assisi and St Clare to many people today.

But those words have also given rise to a great number of questions and debates. Were they meant only for that person on that occasion, or are they meant for all those who are called to consecrated life or for all Christians? Do they propose something which belongs to an individual choice or do they represent an ideal for an entire society? And, in this last case, do they not represent a challenge which is too high for our time, a proposal which has to be considered as Utopian, out of this world, not in line with a society which has chosen the free market?

What kind of modern economy, in fact, could be compatible with these words? Do they not imply a total ignorance of economic processes, a dangerous simplification of the problem of poverty?

These words of Jesus have had a negative reception since the beginning. The first one who heard them was not able to accept them. The Gospel says that 'on hearing these words, his face fell and he went away sorrowful, for he was a man of great wealth'. So we see that our modern difficulties are old. And Jesus underlines this problem by saying: 'How hard it is for those who have riches to enter the kingdom of God!' And the disciples were shocked.

In fact, the words of Jesus are like a thorn in the flesh of every Christian, of all times and of every human society. They confront us with very hard and serious questions, which are at the root of our present painful dissatisfaction with the state of things in this world and which have been

8

the object of international consideration at the United Nations Social Development Summit in Copenhagen in 1995. They are the questions of poverty at the planetary level, of an unjust distribution of riches in our world, of a different style of life forced on people by man's pollution of the earth, and so on.

In this context I shall limit myself to a few reflections on the text.

1 The quoted words of Jesus were never meant to be and were never understood as a solution to social problems. They were first meant as a personal call to a young person to follow Jesus as a disciple, travelling with him solely to dedicate his entire life to the Gospel. They were not a definition of the Christian life as such. They were a personal call. As such they have been heard by many other people and, in the history of the Church, they have inspired the generosity of men and women who gave up everything to dedicate their lives to the service of God and to the service of the poor.

2 But these words are not meant only for *some* people as if it were possible for all the others to forget their fundamental nature or to treat them superficially. They speak to everyone and to all society.

3 These words of Jesus are not a condemnation of riches as such. In the Old Testament, wealth was not condemned, provided that it was shared. It was considered as a sign that a person was faithful to God and was blessed. So long as someone is not liberated from the urgency and concern of material needs, it is difficult for him to be free and open to higher values.

4 But Jesus knows that freedom does not come as such through liberation from material needs. Needs tend to

grow and to create dependency. Riches and the mentality they bring tend to make people spiritually blind, to confuse false and true values. And the confusion that affects the judgment of an individual, to blind him to his own egoism, can also affect a group, can affect an entire society. The society becomes materialistic, blind to values which are not for the benefit of the group. The group feelings can mobilise judgments that put no limits to a group's pretensions . . . And both the individual and the group can claim that their egoism is reasonable, practical, the only commonsense way of acting (cf. R.M. Liddy, 'Lonergan on the Catholic University', *Method*, Journal of Lonergan Studies, 7, 1989, p. 123). The materialistic way of acting becomes a philosophy.

5 What Jesus proposes to the rich young man and through him, he suggests, to each one of us, is exactly the opposite: freedom of heart, liberation from the slavery of earthly desires and true concern for others, that freedom of heart which is at the root of the possibility of sharing. This doctrine is valid not only for individuals, but also for nations and for all peoples. True concern for social justice, care for the poor and the needy, to be open to the problems of other nations and especially the south of the world, the quest for a universal social order which could foster a new 'civilisation of love', to quote the words of Pope Paul VI, all these things derive from those five little words which Jesus proposed to an unknown young man two thousand years ago. They are the same values which guide us in search of a European unity, which has to be not only a financial and economic unity, a unity of the market, but a unity grounded on spiritual values and open to the rest of the world.

Out of these values a rich tradition of solidarity has been born and developed in this country, both within and outside the Christian Churches. We can think of the Anti-Slavery Movement, Christian Aid, the Catholic Fund for Overseas Development (CAFOD), and many other institutions. It is also out of these Christian values that fifty years ago Britain 'stood alone' in the face of the Nazi onslaught and came to victory.

Cardinal Cahal Brendan Daly

Archbishop of Armagh

Cahal Brendan Daly was born in 1917 in Loughguile, County Antrim, Northern Ireland. He was educated at St Patrick's National School, Loughguile; St Malachy's College, Belfast; Queen's University, Belfast and the Institut Catholique, Paris. He received his Licentiate in Theology in 1942, his Doctorate in Theology in 1944 and his Licentiate in Philosophy in 1953. He was ordained priest in 1941, and ordained Bishop in 1967 when he was Bishop of Ardagh and Clonmaconis until 1982 when he became Bishop of Down and Connor until 1990. On 6 December 1990 he became Archbishop of Armagh and Primate of All-Ireland. He was appointed to the College of Cardinals in 1991.

At various times he has been Classics Master in St Malachy's College, Belfast, lecturer and reader at Queen's University; Belfast. He was also a founder member of the 'Christus Rex Society' for the study of social problems in the light of Christian social teaching. He is a former Chairman of the Advisory Committee on Sacred Art and Architecture to the Irish Commission for Liturgy, former Chairman of the Episcopal Commission on Catechetics, and a member of the Pontifical Council for promoting Christian Unity.

He speaks French fluently with comprehension and reading knowledge of Italian, some reading knowledge of German, together with Latin and Greek. He is the author of several books, the latest being *Northern Ireland – Peace – Now is the Time* which was published in 1994. Many of his pastoral letters to the Diocese of Down and Connor and the Archdiocese of Armagh have been published and widely distributed.

13

Cardinal Cahal Brendan Daly
Archbishop of Armagh

Jesus meets the woman taken in adultery:
touching the lives of sinners

(John 8:1–11)

2

There have been at various times in the history of the Christian Church people who strongly resisted the very idea of forgiveness for grave sins committed after baptism. There have indeed been people who held that grave sin was totally incompatible with membership of the Christian Church. For these, the Church was the Church of the 'Pure Ones'; this was the very name taken by the Cathars, in the early Middle Ages. Puritanism, under various titles and in different guises, has often raised its head down the Christian centuries. An early Christian writer of North Africa, Tertullian, was one such person. A man of brilliant intellect, but sadly of disputatious and intolerant disposition, he began by vigorously defending the Church's right to forgive sins, but later, even more vehemently, denied that the Church had any such right. His growing rigorism caused him to abandon the Catholic Church and to join the sect of the Montanists. Eventually he seceded from them and founded a sect of his own. In fact, denial of the possibility of forgiveness for sins has always ended in the formation of a heretical sect outside the community of the Catholic Church. People who claim to be more Catholic than the Church often end by finding themselves outside of it.

The Church and Sin

It should be remembered, however, that there was in the early centuries of the Church an inclination towards believing that a person who committed grave sin after

15

baptism could not be forgiven. Baptism was the sacrament of forgiveness, and all past sins were obliterated in the waters of the font, for the person who entered those waters in faith and repentance. This was one primary meaning of the baptismal theme, stressed by St Paul, of 'dying' in baptism with Christ who conqered sin in his Passion, and then 'rising' with Christ to a new life in which the past and the world, with all its sinful ways, would be banished for ever. The call of baptism was a call to holiness, to sainthood. In the New Testament and in the early Church, Christians were called simply 'saints'. When St Paul was writing a letter to one of his Christian communities, he addressed it to 'the saints', or 'the saints of God' at Corinth, Ephesus, Philippi, or wherever.

The baptised in the early Church were usually adult converts, who had been led by the announcement of the Good News to faith in Jesus Christ and had been drawn by his grace to renounce their pagan past, with its sin and its spiritual darkness, and to commit their lives from that moment to Jesus Christ as their personal Lord and Saviour, and to walking in his way and in his light. Baptism was called 'enlightenment' and sin 'darkness', and the two seemed utterly irreconcilable.

The theme of light and life as opposed to darkness, sin and death, is found again and again in the New Testament, and particularly in St John's Gospel and in his Letters. In John's first Letter, we read:

This is what we heard from [Jesus Christ] and the message that we are announcing to you: God is light; in him there is no darkness at all (1 John 1:5).

Perhaps the strongest statement in the whole New Testament about the incompatibility of sin with faith and baptism is found in the Letter to the Hebrews:

If, after we have been given knowledge of the truth, we should deliberately commit any sins, then there is no longer any sacrifice for them. There will be left only the dreadful prospect of judgment . . . Anyone who tramples on the Son of God, and who treats the blood of the Covenant which sanctified him as if it were not holy, and who insults the Spirit of grace, will be condemned to a far severer punishment (Heb. 10:26–9).

St Paul repeats a similar message again and again. In the sixth chapter of his Letter to the Romans, we read:

When we were baptised we went into the tomb with [Christ] and joined him in death, so that as Christ was raised from the dead by the Father's glory, we too might live a new life . . . When a person dies, of course, he or she has finished with sin . . . When [Christ] died, he died, once for all, to sin, so his life now is life with God; and in that way, you too must consider yourselves to be dead to sin but alive for God in Christ Jesus . . . That is why you must not let sin reign in your mortal bodies . . . why you must not let any part of your body turn into an unholy weapon fighting on the side of sin; instead . . . you should make every part of your body into a weapon fighting on the side of God; and then sin will no longer dominate your life, since you are living by grace and not by law' (Rom. 6:3–4, 10–11, 13–14).

In the Letter to the Ephesians, Paul says:

You were dead through the crimes and the sins in which you used to live when you were following the way of this world . . . We all were among them too in the past, living sensual lives, ruled entirely by our own physical desires

17

and our own ideas . . . I want to urge you in the name of the Lord, not to go on living the aimless kind of life that pagans live. Intellectually, they are in the dark, and they are estranged from the life of God . . . Their sense of right and wrong once dulled, they have abandoned themselves to sexuality and eagerly pursue a career of indecency of every kind. Now that is hardly the way you have learned from Christ . . . You must give up your old way of life; you must put aside your old self, which gets corrupted by following illusory desires. Your mind must be renewed by a spiritual revolution, so that you can put on the new self, that has been created in God's way, in the holiness of the truth (Eph. 4:17–24).

Writing to the Colossians, Paul says:

You must kill everything in you that belongs only to earthly life: fornication, impurity, guilty passion, evil desires, and especially greed, which is the same thing as worshipping a false god; all this is the sort of behaviour that makes God angry. And this is the way in which you used to live when you were surrounded by people doing the same thing; but now you, of all people, must give all these things up: being bad-tempered, spitefulness, abusive language and dirty talk; and never tell each other lies. You have stripped off your old behaviour with your old self, and you put on a new self which will progress towards true knowledge the more it is renewed in the image of its creator (Col. 3:5–10).

In principle then, sin should not have a place in the life of the Christian. In practice, however, human nature is weak and frail, and sin remains a permanent possibility and a persistent reality in the lives of Christians. From the outset, the Church had to reflect on the question of whether and how Christians who sinned could continue to be part of the family of the Church. This reflection had naturally to be guided by what the Church read and meditated in its founding and defining documents, the Sacred Scriptures, the Word of God.

The Lord and Forgiveness of Sin

The fact is that both the condemnation of sin and the forgiveness of sinners are equally stressed in both the Old Testament, and particularly in the New. Here, side by side with the uncompromising rejection of sin, we find an even stronger insistence on the mercy and forgiveness of God. The first recorded word of Jesus in his public life is the word: 'Repent'. This is inseparably linked with faith in him: 'Repent and believe the Good News' (Mark 1:15). The Good News is precisely the news that sins are forgiven by the coming into our world of Jesus, the Christ, the Son of God. In the New Testament, we find that, while Jesus alone among human beings has God's exclusive power to forgive sins, the ministry of forgiveness is also entrusted by him to the Church. This ministry is first imparted to Peter separately, and then to the apostles collectively. In St Matthew's sixteenth chapter, Jesus says to Peter in the presence of the other disciples:

> You are Peter and on this rock I will build my church . . . I will give you the keys of the kingdom of heaven; whatever you bind upon earth shall be considered bound in heaven; whatever you loose on earth shall be considered loosed in heaven (Matt 16: 17–19).

In the eighteenth chapter of the same Gospel, the ministry of forgiveness is entrusted by Christ to the Church represented by the disciples collectively; and the same formula is used as that already used in the case of Peter (cf. Matt. 18:18).

After the resurrection, the Lord, about to take leave in visible form of the Church, his 'little flock', met the disciples in the upper room and said to them:

> As the Father sent me
> so am I sending you.

Then He breathed upon them and said:

> Receive the Holy Spirit.
> For those whose sins you forgive
> they are forgiven;
> For those whose sins you retain
> they are retained (John 20: 21–3).

St Luke records the risen Lord as giving the disciples a last instruction in which he explained how the promise of the Scriptures had been fulfilled in his person. He said to them:

So you see how it is written that Christ would suffer and on the third day rise from the dead, and that in his name repentance for the forgiveness of sins would be preached to all the nations (Luke 24: 47–8).

In the same instruction, Jesus promised that He would send the Holy Spirit from the Father upon the infant Church, a promise fulfilled at Pentecost.

Since Pentecost the task of the Church has been, on the one hand to proclaim firmly and patiently that its members are called to leave sin behind and lead lives of holiness and, on the other hand, to preach tirelessly and compassionately to sinners the need to repent and the possibility of being repeatedly forgiven. Both messages are entrusted to the Church by the same Jesus Christ.

St John expresses this two-fold imperative in his first Letter. He writes:

> If we say we have no sin in us
> we are deceiving ourselves
> and refusing to admit the truth;
> but if we acknowledge our sins
> then God who is faithful and just
> will forgive our sins and purify us
> from everything that is wrong (1 John 1:8–9).

In the same Letter, his message is:

> I am writing this, my children,
> to stop you sinning;
> but if anyone should sin
> we have our advocate with the Father,
> Jesus Christ, who is just;
> He is the sacrifice that takes our sins away,
> and not only ours,
> but the sins of the whole world (1 John 2:1–2).

There is admittedly an apparent tension between the two truths: first, the principle that the Christian, called to saintliness, should not sin; second, the fact that Christians do go on sinning, and yet can still go on being forgiven. Again and again throughout history, the Church is criticised by some for being too rigorist and by others for being too liberal, castigated by some for being too 'hard-line' in condemning sin, and by others for being too 'soft' in granting forgiveness. The criticism continues in our own time. G. K. Chesterton once remarked that there must be something quite special and unique about an institution which is always being criticised, but whose critics condemn it for opposite and contradictory reasons. This, indeed, was one of the aspects of the Church which led to Chesterton's conversion.

As I have remarked, drawing out the practical conse-quences of this two-fold truth of sin and of forgiveness was not without controversy, both in the early and in the later Church. Again and again, there have been tensions between rigorists and laxists, between puritans and what we now call 'liberals'. The comfort for the Church is that it is preaching what Christ preached and doing what Christ did and is being criticised for precisely the same reasons as Christ was vilified, for being 'the friend of sinners', and, at the same time, the one who condemned sin. The juxtaposition of pulpits and confessional is the Church's way of reconciling, as Christ did, truth with love. It is the Church's way of being faithful, as Christ was, both to divine justice and to the divine mercy.

The woman taken in adultery

This in fact is the meaning of the story recounted in the Gospel passage, the story of the woman caught in the act of adultery. There is debate among scholars as to whether the passage belongs properly to St John's Gospel or has been later attached to the fourth Gospel from a different source. The style of the passage resembles St Luke more than St John and, indeed, it would seem to fit more easily into the fifteenth chapter of St Luke, with its three beautiful parables of God's mercy: the lost sheep, the lost coin and the prodigal son. There is general agreement that the passage is a very early text contemporaneous with the Gospels, and accepted as canonical Scripture, at least as early as St Jerome and the Latin Vulgate translation of the Greek New Testament. Its placing at this point of the

Gospel of St John is natural enough, because the narrative fits into the context of the theme of judgment, which is the theme of the rest of the chapter of St John where the text is now found.

It is not too far-fetched to suggest that the textual problem with the passage could have arisen because some of the rigorists of the early Church tried to exclude the passage from the manuscripts, because they objected to the Lord's message of forgiveness for the heinous and shameful sin of adultery committed by a woman. There are other examples of passages telling of Christ's mercy and compassion for sinners which offended the pious ears of early purists and were excised by them from some manuscripts.

Indeed, the attitude of some early Christian puritans is not too different from that of the 'scribes and pharisees' who brought the woman to Jesus. The woman had been 'caught' in the act of adultery, presumably by two witnesses, for this was the legal requirement for the sentence of death by stoning, prescribed for such a crime in the Mosiac Law, as we find it set out in Deuteronomy 22:21 (cf. Ezek. 16: 38–40). This was a strongly male-centred part of the Old Law; it is notable that there is no mention either in the Law or in this Gospel passage about the male partner in the act of adultery. Here, as elsewhere, Jesus is shown as transcending the male-centredness of the Hebrew culture of his time and as showing particular concern and equal and indeed special respect for women. This aspect of the case is clearly not absent from the minds of the scribes and pharisees who had hauled the woman before Jesus. Their purpose was to trap Jesus into defiance of the Law, and presumably into the scandal of taking the side of a shameless woman against the Law of Moses.

The woman is made to 'stand there in the full view of everybody'. This is the position required for the accused in a case of judicial examination. We find a parallel in the emergency 'court' set up for the trial of Peter and the disciples in Acts 4:7. The phrase calls attention, however, also to the humiliation of the poor woman, surrounded by men who despised the sinner, treated her like the dirt they felt her to be, gloated over her detection 'in flagrante delicto', in the lack of shame of an adulterous act, and who exulted also in the cleverness of the trap they had set for Jesus and at the prospect of finally discrediting him for condoning the scandal of this wanton woman. Clearly, the reputation of Jesus for mercy towards sinners is the motive for their ploy. If that mercy could be shown to amount to encouragement for adulterous behaviour, the name of Jesus would be for ever associated, they reckoned, with moral laxness and decadence. Jesus was obviously not exempt from the misrepresentation and obloquy later to be heaped on some of his followers in later centuries, whose intention was to reach out and touch with compassion the lives of sinners, while never in the slightest way to approve of or to condone their sin.

As soon as the accusers had made their seemingly unanswerable charges against the woman, Jesus began 'writing on the ground with his finger'. There has been much discussion about the meaning of this gesture. Details of an apparently banal nature like this one are rarely recounted in the gospels without some symbolic meaning related to the teaching contained in the narrative. Jesus in this narrative is being tested on his fidelity to what 'Moses has ordered in the Law'. I am inclined to look in this gesture of Jesus for a relevance to this central point in the ploy to trap him. I am inclined to look for other instances in the Bible where God is described as writing with his finger. I find two such instances and they both relate to the writing of the Law by the finger of God on the two stone tablets of the Law (Exod. 31:18; Deut.

9:10; see also Exod. 32:16 and 34:1). These allusions to the 'stone tablets' could scarcely have been lost on experts on the Bible and the Law like the 'scribes and Pharisees'. I believe that Jesus is here telling them that he is the finger of God who wrote the Law which they are accusing him of breaking. He had once declared that it was by the finger of God that he himself cast out devils (Luke 11:20).

Then come the well-known words of Jesus:

If there is any of you who has not sinned, let him be the first to throw a stone at her (v. 7).

The phrase about 'casting the first stone' has entered into common speech and is often used by people who have no idea where the phrase comes from. Challenged in this way and in the face of one claiming such awesome authority as Jesus, the accusers 'went away one by one, beginning with the eldest'. After they all slunk away the woman is left alone with Jesus.

We can try to enter into her feelings at that moment of aloneness. I imagine that she would have been less unhappy if the men had stayed; for even their sneering contempt was less painful for her than the thought of being left alone with Jesus, the 'holy one of God'. Contempt was hurtful, but being left alone with the sinless one was much more to be feared. As the last accuser left, the moment she was dreading came. There was no one there any more between her and Jesus. The gospel story gives the primacy to Jesus at this point: 'Jesus was left alone with the woman', it says. The woman had at last to lift her head and look into his eyes. She must have expected a judgment, a condemnation, a rejection, even more hurtful than the taunts and jibes of the scribes and Pharisees.

Instead, to her amazement, what she sees in the eyes of Jesus is love, respect, a sense of her worth as a person. A woman who had felt used, treated as a thing, a disposable plaything, a sexual object, now feels, perhaps for the first time in her life, that she is a person, respected, valued, healed and indeed loved. Where harsh and heartless condemnation only submerged her heart in hopeless self-loathing and self-pity, the love and respect and mercy which she encountered in the eyes of Jesus evoked deep and loving repentance and brought a sense of hope and new beginning. As St Augustine put it in almost untranslatable Latin: '*Relicti sunt duo: misera et misericordia*' – 'Two were left there alone with one another: misery before mercy; a woman filled with misery before her Saviour filled with mercy.'

It is never a question of her sin's being condoned or treated as trivial and unimportant. On the contrary, love and forgiveness reveal to her the ugliness and evil of her sin, as no scolding or anger could ever have done. Forgiveness gives her the motive for turning away from sin so as to walk in love, the love revealed to her in the eyes of Jesus. From then on, she could never forget his words:

Neither do I condemn you; go away and do not sin any more (v. 11).

The Sacrament of Reconciliation

This narrative of the woman taken in adultery is rich in teaching both for the sinners which we all are and for the exercise of the ministry of reconciliation which Christ has entrusted to his Church. One of the great worries in the Church today is the decline in recourse to the sacrament of penance or reconciliation. Fewer and fewer people are now going to confession, and one wonders what are the causes of this decline and what are its implications. It would seem that the sense of sin has weakened and that people are less aware of the need for confession and less convinced of the relevance of sacramental absolution.

The big worry is that this could indicate a weakening in the sense of God. It is understandable that those who have had the strongest awareness of God and who have committed their lives most to seeking union with God, namely the saints, have been those most conscious of their own sinfulness and of the need for conversion, repentance and forgiveness. We have seen that the call to repentance and to the need for forgiveness was the first call of Jesus as he began his ministry in Galilee. Jesus is promised in the Old Testament and is presented in the New as above all the Saviour who comes to take away our sins. If we do not feel the need to be freed from our sins, then we are scarcely ready to receive Jesus as our Saviour. Awareness of and confession of our need for forgiveness are central to our faith in Jesus Christ. We begin every Mass with the rite of penance: 'As we prepare to celebrate the sacred mysteries, let us call to mind our sins.' If this rite of penance is taken seriously, it should surely lead us to feel the need for that special preparation for the eucharist which is the sacrament of penance.

It is significant also that people who feel no inclination to confess their sins to a priest will have no hesitation in confessing their most intimate lives and relationships to 'agony aunts' or chat show presenters, and to do this, not in the secrecy of the confessional, but openly before the public. There would seem to be some innate need to confess, and indeed to confess to other human beings, and nevertheless a lack of conviction about the need or value of confessing to a priest.

There is even a kind of secular analogue to awareness of the need to be forgiven and to be healed of one's fault, existing side by side with neglect of the Church's sacrament of forgiveness and healing. It is accepted in the secular domain that one cannot be successfully treated of compulsive abuse of alcohol or other forms of substance abuse until one acknowledges that one has an addiction and accepts the need to be helped. Acceptance of one's own helplessness and one's need for healing is a precondition for change of deviant and destructive behaviour in many other areas also of what is called 'inappropriate behaviour'.

If there is a human need for confession, and if it is a precondition of healing that one first accepts one's own powerlessness, then surely it can only be weakness of faith which causes us to neglect the confession offered by the Church and the help of divine grace, which is available in the sacrament of penance. In the sacrament of penance, one is coming to the only Power that can lift us up in our powerlessness, the only Healer who can cure our most distressing afflictions, the only Saviour who can deliver us from our spiritual illness. He is Jesus Christ, our only Saviour. The priest in the sacrament of penance is his representative. It is alone with Jesus Christ himself that we kneel or sit in confession, our misery face to face with his mercy, like the woman taken in adultery. Only he can send us away in peace, with the knowledge that our sins are forgiven, that we are accepted and loved in spite of the mess that we constantly make of our own lives. The words of absolution spoken by the priest in the name of Jesus Christ and of his Church assure us of pardon and peace, which are, each of them, the fruit of the experience of being loved, as the sinful woman knew that she was looked at with love by Jesus Christ when left face to face with him, her misery healed by his mercy.

Every confession room contains a crucifix. We have only to look at the crucifix to know how desperately we are wanted and needed and loved by God. This is what Christ was prepared to go through for me; this is what I mean to him. This, St Paul tells us, is what the teaching of love means. One writer has remarked that the woman taken in adultery was freed from execution because Jesus was willing to be executed on the Cross in her place. The Cure of Ars, the great confessor of the last century, said that every time we receive absolution we take Jesus down from the Cross and take him into our arms and hold him close to our heart as Mary did on Calvary.

Elie Weisel was in Auchwitz as a young boy in 1945 when the Nazis hanged a boy of fourteen and forced all the inmates of the camp to file past his little body as it turned and twisted, hanging in agony from the tree. Someone shouted: 'Where is God now?' The Christian must answer: 'He is hanging there from that tree for us all, for me.' As St Paul said: 'He loved me and delivered himself for me.' Christ on the Cross looks on me as I kneel or sit before his crucifix in confession. He looks at me with eyes of unbelievable love. The eyes of love, they say, are blind; the loved one is transformed by their very look. That is why we can go away from confession with a feeling of peace which no human therapy can ever give, but only the words of Jesus himself, speaking through his priest: 'Go in peace, your sins are forgiven.'

Cardinal Adrianus Johannes Simonis

Archbishop of Utrecht

Adrianus Johannes Simonis was born in 1931 at Lisse in the Netherlands. Between 1945 and 1957 he was educated at Gymnasium, Minor-Seminary Hageveld Heemstede and Major-Seminary Warmond. He was ordained priest in 1957 and spent a year as Catholic chaplain in Waddinxveen and a year as Catholic chaplain in Rotterdam. Between 1959 and 1966 he studied at the Pontifical Biblical Institute in Rome and the Institute for Biblical Sciences in Jerusalem.

He gained his PhD in Theology in 1966. From 1966 to 1970 he was Catholic chaplain in The Hague and in 1966 became a member of the Cathedral Chapter. In 1970 he became a Member of the Diocesan Pastoral Council and, until 1983, Bishop of Rotterdam. In 1983 he became Bishop of Utrecht and he became a Cardinal in 1985. He has also been awarded a Knighthood in the order of the Dutch Lion.

Cardinal Adrianus J Simonis
Archbishop of Utrecht

Jesus meets the Pharisees:
confronting hatred in society

(Mark 2:13–17,23–3:6)

3

When I was assigned the topic of 'Jesus meets the Pharisees; confronting hatred in society' I felt it was a difficult theme, because the Gospel does not really offer us a closed system of thought, but rather challenges us time and again to think about certain things.

The topic is especially difficult, because it is practically impossible to consider Phariseeism in an objective way. Phariseeism is a matter of all times and ages, and is to be found in every human heart, under the guise of deceptive appearances and fine words, but an attitude to life that does not really correspond with these. It seemed best to me, therefore, to consider with you a number of Gospel passages, in order to meditate on the question of who I am, and how I might be able to grow towards that purity of heart which Jesus presents to us as ideal. 'Blessed are the pure of heart, for they will see God.' May God's Spirit of truth enlighten us.

One of the best-known stories about Jesus and the Pharisees is a story in which Jesus himself does not appear, except as the story-teller. It is the parable that we find in the Gospel of St Luke about the Pharisee and the tax collector.

Two men went up into the temple to pray, one a Pharisee and the other a tax collector. The Pharisee stood and prayed thus with himself, 'God, I thank thee that I am not like other men, extortioners, unjust, adulterers, or even like this tax collector. I fast twice a week, I give tithes of all that I get.' But the tax collector, standing far off, would not even lift up his eyes to heaven, but beat his breast, saying, 'God, be merciful to me a sinner!' I tell you, this man went down to his house justified rather than the other (Luke 18:10–14, RSV).

We hear from St Luke that Jesus told this parable 'to some who trusted in themselves that they were righteous and despised others' (v. 9), Luke does not say that Jesus directed this parable specifically at the Pharisees. Rather, we may assume that Luke leaves the interpretation of the parable to his readers. In fact, I think that quite a few of us have felt a little uncomfortable at times when this story was told. Of course, there will be some people who cheerfully identify themselves with the tax collector, even if he calls himself a sinner, either because, in this story, he appears to be the 'good guy' or because they have always heard that the Pharisees were to be despised as thoroughly bad guys. But, is this not precisely a story about those who despise other people? Consequently many are embarrassed, because they honestly do not know whether they would prefer to be identified with the Pharisee or with the tax collector. It is the 'embarrassment of choice', which is the birthright of every human being and which cannot be taken away from us by any system of ethics.

Let us look at some of the stories in which Jesus himself meets the Pharisees. These stories are not about a struggle for political or economic power, but about fundamental ethical and theological issues. Nevertheless, the subtitle of this chapter, 'Confronting hatred in society', is quite apt. On the one hand, the process of the origin and development of hostility, in society as well as in personal relationships, is much the same. On the other hand, many political and economic struggles also contain an ethical or even a religious element.

Several of the stories about the encounters between Jesus and the Pharisees certainly contain elements of hostility, enmity or even outright hatred. The parable of the Pharisee and the tax collector, however, should warn us that it will not be easy to draw from these encounters conclusions that are readily applicable to specific situations in present-day society. For the moment, let us think carefully and meditate quite honestly in ourselves about the questions the encounters of Jesus and the Pharisees put before us. Afterwards let us pray that God may give us some insight that will be fruitful in our encounters.

1   The parable of the Pharisee and the tax collector had its origin in one of the earliest encounters of Jesus with the Pharisees, as the following story from the Gospel of St Mark shows.

> [Jesus] saw Levi the son of Alphaeus sitting at the tax office, and he said to him, 'Follow me.' And he rose and followed him. And as he sat at table in his house, many tax collectors and sinners were sitting with Jesus and his disciples; for there were many who followed him. And the scribes of the Pharisees, when they saw that he was eating with sinners and tax collectors, said to his disciples, 'Why does he eat with tax collectors and sinners?' And when Jesus heard it, he said to them, 'Those who are well have no need of a physician, but those who are sick; I came not to call the righteous, but sinners' (Mark 2:14–17, RSV).

In this story, near the beginning of the public ministry of Jesus, we are already feeling a certain tension in the relationship between Jesus and the Pharisees. We all know that antagonism is not always the result of some specific incident or information. Very often it grows gradually from preconceived ideas, especially when a negative opinion seems to be confirmed or, on the contrary, a positive opinion is contradicted by the behaviour of the person or group concerned. Our first question, therefore, is: what did the main characters of the story know about each other? Were they in any way prejudiced?

From the answer that Jesus gave to the Pharisees – 'I came not to call the righteous, but sinners' it might be deduced that Jesus shared the high opinion that most people of his time had of the Pharisees. At a time when Jesus himself called his contemporaries 'an adulterous and sinful generation' (Mark 8:38) the Pharisees were considered to be righteous men. They upheld the Law as it is found in the five books of Moses with its religious, ethical and social commandments, together with later observances, especially those regarding tithes and the purity and impurity of food. In this respect, they differed not only from tax collectors, as in the parable, but also from the ordinary people, the people of the land, who were not well educated in these matters.

Many Pharisees belonged to a group that undertook to observe meticulously the observances of tithing and of purity and impurity. This resulted in a certain barrier between the Pharisees and ordinary people. It should, however, not be compared with apartheid. Pharisees never were a social class; they came from all strata of society, so this barrier never gave rise to a social rift or to mutual hostility. On the contrary, although few in number, the Pharisees had considerable religious and social influence among the people. The learned scribes, especially, were an indispensable element of every community as lawyers and teachers of the Law, which was in fact both religious and civil law. On the other hand, the story tells us nothing about any prejudice the Pharisees may have had about Jesus, except that he was not a Pharisee. They had heard about Jesus's teaching in the synagogue in Capernaum as one who had authority, and not as the scribes' (Mark 1:22) and possibly some of them knew of Jesus's relationship with the group of John the Baptist in Judea. The only thing we do know is what Mark tells us: the scribes of the Pharisees saw that Jesus was eating with sinners and tax collectors. Sinners, of course, were those who were publicly known to be sinners, as in the parable: extortioners, the unjust, adulterers, or even like this tax collector (Luke 18:11). This caused them to question his disciples, 'why does he eat with tax collectors and sinners?'(Mark 2:16).

Let us, therefore, leave the question of prejudice aside and concentrate on the scene as it is described in Mark. There is a great contrast. On one side of the picture we see Jesus and his disciples sitting among a group of tax collectors and sinners, eating together. As in nearly every culture, eating together suggests something like a family or a group of friends, people who belong together or who want to be together. On the other side are the Pharisees. Perhaps they are passing in the street at the back of Levi's house, from where they could have a glimpse of the merry party around Jesus. We can picture the scribes, as in an earlier story, of Jesus healing a paralytic in his home in Capernaum, where Mark has observed them: 'some of the scribes were sitting there, questioning in their hearts' (Mark 2:6 cf. Luke 5:1) They are sitting there, as in judgment, but it seems that each one of them is alone with his own thoughts.

Then the silence between the groups is broken by a question, just as in the earlier story. There it was Jesus who asked the question: 'Why do you question thus in your hearts? (v. 8). This time the question comes from the Pharisees, but again they dare not confront Jesus himself. Instead they address his disciples: 'Why does he eat with tax collectors and sinners?' (v. 16). The answer is quite simple: I eat with them, because they need me. They need me, because they are morally ill. They need someone who is prepared to heal them, as I healed the man who was physically and morally sick. I see it as my calling to heal all those who are not so well integrated in our society as you are, because you are already living, or at least pretending to live lives that are pleasing to God.

This simple story of one of the first encounters of Jesus and the Pharisees gives ample food for thought. Even if hostility is caused by a specific incident, this is generally because of preconceived ideas about certain groups of people. We are all familiar with this phenomenon. But are we always aware of the fact that such groups often do not exist in reality, but only in our minds, because we are grouping certain people together? The Pharisees were real groups, who had formed a moral kinship; for that reason they were grouped together by other people. Sinners and tax collectors were grouped together by other people as well, as outsiders, and for this reason they came together, in search of companionship.

People want to know where a person belongs, very often in order to know where they themselves belong. It is a function of the human mind always to classify, to arrange things in an orderly manner, to put labels on other people. This is what the Pharisees were doing when they asked: 'Why does he eat with tax collectors and sinners?' There is nothing wrong with this natural disposition, because it may help people to find their place in society, but sometimes it keeps people separate, rather than bringing them together. It is never easy to judge people adequately and fairly.

This brings us to another point in the story. Very often a judgment is based on insufficient information. Accordingly it seems right and proper that the Pharisees should ask the question: why does he eat with tax collectors and sinners? However, should they not have addressed their question to Jesus himself rather than to his disciples? (It may seem the same thing happens in 2:18ff, when the people ask Jesus why his disciples do not fast. There, however, one could argue that, as the teacher, Jesus is responsible for the actions of his disciples.) This is what happens quite often: people are afraid of asking a direct question, of entering into a discussion, because they want to avoid a confrontation that could become unpleasant or even hostile. In the next chapter of the Gospel of Mark we shall see the tragic consequences of such an attitude.

Finally we have to consider Jesus's answer to the question of the Pharisees. Most of us, I suppose, are prejudiced in favour of Jesus, so we think it a marvellous answer. 'I do not look upon these people', Jesus seems to say, 'from the point of view of a lawyer, but in the way in which a physician treats his patients.' (Such a proverb seems to have been well known in circles of Greek philosophers; see the commentaries.) But is this a true answer to the question? I do not mean whether the answer is historically true or theologically true, as it certainly is for us Christians, but whether it could satisfy the Pharisees, who wanted to avoid every contact with unclean foodstuffs and unclean people, because they considered this the will of God as expressed in Scripture. At this point in the Gospel Mark does not tell us about any reaction of the Pharisees and, although there is a suggestion of mounting tension, there is as yet no open confrontation.

Presently we shall return to Mark, but first we shall look at another encounter between Jesus and the Pharisees, because it is always wise to look at a possible conflict from different angles.

2   The story in Mark shows Jesus sitting at table with tax collectors and sinners, whereas the Pharisees are passing in the street. Luke knows this particular story

too (5:29–32) but he also tells a story in which the scene
is reversed (7:36–50). This story is much more detailed
than the other one, and it begins:

> One of the Pharisees asked him [Jesus] to eat with him,
> and he went into the Pharisee's house, and took his place
> at table. And behold, a woman of the city, who was a
> sinner, when she learned that he was at table in the
> Pharisee's house, brought an alabaster flask of ointment,
> and standing behind him at his feet, weeping, she began
> to wet his feet with her tears, and wiped them with her
> hair, and kissed his feet, and anointed them with the
> ointment. Now when the Pharisee who had invited him
> saw it, he said to himself, 'If this man were a prophet,
> he would have known who and what sort of woman this
> is who is touching him, for she is a sinner' (vv. 36–9).

Before we move on to the really interesting part of the
story, the conversation between Jesus and the Pharisee,
we shall have to ask a few obvious questions. The first
question is: why did the Pharisee invite Jesus to dinner?
Either he did not know about Jesus's eating with tax
collectors and sinners, or he did not think that a serious
impediment. In any case, he was not familiar with Jesus,
because he thought about him as 'this man'. He must,
however, have heard about him, because he addressed
him as 'Teacher'. Did he invite Jesus, together with other
guests, out of simple curiosity, perhaps mixed with a
certain self-importance, or did he have an ulterior motive
and want to test him?

The second question is more difficult to answer: why and
how did the woman come into the house of the Pharisee and
even into the room where the Pharisee was dining with his
guests? She was known in the town as 'a sinner'. She need
not have been a prostitute, but could have been a woman

whose marriage, for instance, was not in accordance with the Law. She must have heard that Jesus was a guest in the house of the Pharisee, because she brought the flask of ointment with her. The Pharisee must have been a well-to-do man, just like the tax collector Levi in the other story. Perhaps he left the back-door open so that the people of the town could have a look into his patio and see a glimpse of his famous guest. In this way the woman may have slipped into the open patio and past the kitchen, perhaps in the wake of the women serving at table. If, as was the custom in antiquity, Jesus was lying on his side in the place of honour, opposite his host, his feet were close to the open patio, and the woman had every opportunity to do what she had set out to do, for whatever reason she wanted to do it.

The setting of the story would have been much more familiar to the people who first heard it than to us, but the actions of the woman and the conversation that followed would have been just as surprising to them as to the guests of the Pharisee.

This time Jesus took the initiative. As Luke has pictured the scene, Jesus did not even need his supernatural knowledge to know what the Pharisee was thinking. One look at his face would have been enough for anyone to know what was in his mind. Jesus tells a story:

'Simon, I have something to say to you.' And he answered, 'What is it, Teacher?' 'A certain creditor had two debtors; one owed five hundred denarii, and the other fifty. When they could not pay, he forgave them both. Now, which of them will love him more?' Simon answered, 'The one, I suppose, to whom he forgave more' (vv. 40–3).

Of course, this story should be taken as a parable, but in itself its meaning could not have been clear to the Pharisee and his guests. Therefore Jesus explained its meaning in a very direct way:

> Then, turning toward the woman he said to Simon, 'Do you see this woman? I entered your house, you gave me no water for my feet, but she has wet my feet with her tears and wiped them with her hair. You gave me no kiss, but from the time I came in she has not ceased to kiss my feet. You did not anoint my head with oil, but she has anointed my feet with ointment' (vv. 44–6).

Simon must have been terribly embarrassed. Jesus reproached him for something that, at least in certain circles, is considered to be worse than sin – bad manners. In Israel hospitality was a moral obligation of the highest order, the mark of a really pious man, especially when shown towards strangers and weary travellers. As in our own society, there were no specific rules, only some conventions. Sincere hospitality depends on the way a guest is made to feel welcome. Now, imagine Simon at the moment when Jesus entered his house. He certainly wanted to show off the famous, but – according to some of his colleagues – disreputable rabbi as a guest, but he did not want to treat him as an honoured guest or even as a friend. He ushered him quickly into the dining room, without offering to let his servants wash his feet, which in their light sandals were, of course, dirty from the street, and without offering perfumed ointment for his hair, which would have been nice for his neighbours at table. Perhaps he used the excuse that the other guests were waiting. Simon certainly did not want to kiss Jesus, because such a kiss would mean either that he considered Jesus as in some way his superior, or that he welcomed him as an intimate friend.

Jesus, however, did not reproach Simon, because he was offended. Rather, he wanted to show him and the other guests the real meaning of the parable he had just told.

Therefore I tell you, her sins, which are many, are forgiven, for she loved much; but he who is forgiven little, loves little (v. 47).

The parable simply applies an everyday human experience to the present situation. People who experience a remission of debts – in whatever sense, but especially in the sense of forgiveness of sins – will be very grateful and will try to show their gratitude. The greater the debt, the greater the gratitude. Simon did not realise that he had broken any of the commandments. He was only embarrassed because his rudeness had been exposed, and he did not even realise that he had been forgiven by his guest. The woman, however, knew she was a sinner in the eyes of God. She knew that she had offended God by breaking his commandments. She may have heard Jesus telling the crowd that God 'is kind to the ungrateful and the selfish. Be merciful even as your Father is merciful' (Luke 6:35–6) or perhaps she had even heard what he said to the paralytic in Capernaum: My son, your sins are forgiven' (Mark 2:5) She really came to believe that God was prepared to grant forgiveness to her, too. By her loving gestures she showed her gratitude in the only way she knew, and Jesus understood.

He said to her: 'Your sins are forgiven.' Then those who were at table with him began to say among themselves, 'Who is this, who even forgives sins?' (Luke 7:49).

They did not understand that God had forgiven the woman, because they did not see an act of repentance. They could only think in rigid categories. Jesus, however, saw that she wanted to trust in God and he said to her: 'Your faith has saved you; go in peace' (v. 50).

Whereas the woman is sent away 'in peace', the Pharisee simply disappears from the story without a word. The whole story illustrates the answer that Jesus gave in the story of Mark, and that we also find in Luke, but with a few extra words:

> Those who are well have no need of a physician, but those who are sick; I came not to call the righteous, but sinners to repentance (Luke 5:31–2).

In a friendly way Jesus exposes the fundamental difference between himself and the Pharisee. The righteous Pharisee is not right in his appraisal of Jesus, nor in his judgment of the woman, because the righteous tend to be inflexible. He knows about God's forgiving the repentant sinner, but he does not recognise repentance, when all he sees is an unbecoming and indecorous act by a person he knows as unrepentant. We shall see more about this fundamental difference when we return to the stories in the Gospel of Mark. There is, however, yet another point to be made. Although we have not witnessed a hostile confrontation in this story, it shows that other psychological factors, in addition to those we have already seen (prejudice and lack of moral courage), can be at the root of growing hostility and can ultimately lead to hatred, embarrassment and discomfort.

3   Most people feel very uncomfortable when they are closely watched. It is a sign of suspicion and often of a certain degree of hostility. As Mark continues his gospel, we notice that such was the attitude taken by the Pharisees.

One sabbath he [Jesus] was going through the grain-fields; and as they made their way his disciples began to pluck heads of grain. And the Pharisees said to him, 'Look, why are they doing what is not lawful on the sabbath?' (2: 23–4).

Let us try once more to imagine the scene. Jesus is walking through the fields outside the town where he was staying. None the less the Pharisees see what the disciples are doing. They must have watched closely and continuously. As Luke puts it: They were 'lying in wait for him, to catch at something he might say', or do (11:54). In answer to the question of the Pharisees, Jesus refers to a well-known story from Scripture.

Have you never read what David did, when he was in need and was hungry, he and those who were with him: how he entered the house of God, when Abiathar was high priest, and ate the bread of the Presence, which it is not lawful for any but the priests to eat, and also gave it to those who were with him? (Mark 2:25–6).

The question whether the disciples really were in need is irrelevant because Jesus does not draw the conclusion that we should expect – need has no law – from the scriptural example. Instead, he goes right to the heart of the matter by giving an answer to a much more fundamental issue: what is the purpose of the law? He states: 'The sabbath was made for man, not man for the sabbath' (v. 27). There is no reaction. It seems that Jesus is able to heal the sick and the sinners, but not the righteous. In the next story Mark confirms this view.

[Jesus] entered the synagogue, and a man was there who had a withered hand. And they watched him, to see whether he would heal him on the sabbath, so that they might accuse him (3:1–2).

Once more Jesus tried to engage the Pharisees in a discussion in their own field:

'Is it lawful on the sabbath to do good or to do harm, to save life or to kill?' But they were silent. And he looked around at them with anger, grieved at their hardness of heart, and said to the man, 'Stretch out your hand.' He stretched it out, and his hand was restored. The Pharisees went out, and immediately held counsel with the Herodians against him, how to destroy him (3:4–6).

In this story we find the climax of Jesus's encounters with the Pharisees in the Gospel of Mark. The Pharisees no longer respond. Mark describes their attitude with a scriptural expression: 'their hardness of heart'. They are like stone. They have closed off every possibility of a reasonable discussion. This, in turn, makes Jesus angry, but his anger is not caused by hostility but rather by grief. It is the same anger that underlies the well-known passage in the Gospel of St Matthew, chapter 23, in which the Pharisees are addressed with a vehement denunciation of their rigidity and hypocrisy:

The scribes and the Pharisees sit on Moses' seat; so practise and observe whatever they tell you, but not what they do; for they preach, but do not practise (vv. 2–3).

We shall look at the reasons for the harsh hostility of the Pharisees presently, but first let us try to reconstruct the process of growing hostility.

As we have seen, the stories of the encounters between Jesus and the Pharisees are not about a struggle for political or economic power, but about fundamental ethical and theological issues. They are not about having rights, but about being right. They are an illustration of people who trust in themselves that they are righteous, and despise others. Differences of opinion, however fundamental they may be, need not lead to enmity, hostility or even hatred, as long as people accept each other as equals. Very often, however, people are uneasy with each other, perhaps because they harbour hidden motives, as in the case of the Pharisee Simon. Uneasiness and embarrassment may cause people to avoid a direct confrontation with each other and to try and get information in a roundabout way. In such a situation a person's mind will be open to the kind of prejudice that can be confirmed quite easily. We are all inclined to put labels on each other anyway. But once people start watching each other closely, in order to confirm existing prejudices, the process that leads to hostility is practically unavoidable. In this process there comes a moment, when a real confrontation, let alone a reasonable discussion of the issue, is no longer possible.

In the story of the healing of the man with a withered hand Mark sketches the climax of the process in just a few strokes: 'they were silent . . . their hardness of heart . . . they went out, and immediately held counsel with the Herodians against him, how to destroy him.'

'They were silent': they had started with questions, but now they no longer wanted to speak. 'Their hardness of heart': they no longer listened. 'They went out': they separated themselves completely and physically from their enemy. 'They held counsel with the Herodians against him'.

(We find this alliance only in Mark, but other Gospels have other alliances, such as with Sadducees, Matt.

16:1, with the lawyers, Luke 5:17, and with the chief priests, John 11:47.) This is an element in the process that we have not yet seen. The Herodians were friends of the tetrarch Herod Antipas, who ruled over Galilee. They were, therefore, not much interested in ethical or theological questions, but concerned with politics. They would have been hostile towards Jesus because of the danger of political unrest in Galilee. Normally the Pharisees would not be friends with the Herodians. It is a sign of the Pharisees' blind hostility towards Jesus, that they associate with such people. 'How to destroy him': in this context the word 'destroy' does not necessarily mean that the Pharisees wanted to kill Jesus, but they wanted to stop Jesus's influence on the people (cf. Paul, who wrote: 'I persecuted the church of God violently and tried to destroy it, Gal. 1:13), although for reasons that were obviously different from those of the Herodians. Let us now try to find an answer to the question: what lay at the root of the hostility of the Pharisees to Jesus?

4   Let us go back once more to Mark and listen to the one story that we have not yet considered.

> Now John's disciples and the Pharisees were fasting; and people came and said to him [Jesus], 'Why do John's disciples and the disciples of the Pharisees fast, but your disciples do not fast?' And Jesus said to them, 'Can the wedding guests fast while the bridegroom is with them? As long as they have the bridegroom with them, they cannot fast. The days will come, when the bridegroom is taken away from them, and then they will fast in that day' (2:18–20).

As we have already seen, Jesus very often responds to a question by telling a parable. When Jesus told this parable, it had a meaning that everyone who was familiar with

Scripture could understand. To give but one example, in the book of the prophet Hosea we find the following passage:

I [the Lord] will make for you [the people] a convenant on that day with the beasts of the field, the birds of the air, and the creeping things of the ground; and I will abolish the bow, the sword, and war from the land; and I will make you lie down in safety. And I will betroth you to me in righteousness and in justice, in steadfast love, and in mercy. I will betroth you to me in faithfulness; and you shall know the Lord. (2:18–20).

Obviously the wedding is a metaphor for the renewal of the covenant between God and his people. Now Mark introduces Jesus at the beginning of his gospel in the following way:

Jesus came into Galilee, preaching the gospel of God, and saying, 'The time is fulfilled, and the kingdom of God is at hand; repent, and believe in the gospel' (1:14–15).

The word 'gospel', as you may know, derives from Old English 'god spell', which means 'good tidings', exactly what it says in the Greek original; these are precisely the good tidings of the fulfilment of God's promise and the coming of the kingdom of God.

Everything is going to be new and there lies the root of the conflict between the Pharisees and Jesus. The Pharisees were concerned with upholding the Law and the traditions of the Fathers. As I have already indicated, we should not think that they, or the rabbis that came after them, were simply rigid and legalistic. They did not apply the Law in a mechanical way, but they tried to interpret and explain the Law in accordance with the situation as they saw it. Only, as Jesus tried to explain in his little parable, the situation itself had changed radically. Within the framework of Jesus's metaphor we can say: we have left everyday life with its restrictions and obligations for the rejoicing of a wedding feast. Immediately after the parable of the wedding, Jesus himself analysed the situation in two more parables taken from everyday life:

No one sews a piece of unshrunk cloth on an old garment; if he does, the patch tears away from it, the new from it, the new from the old, and a worse tear is made. And no one puts new wine into old wineskins; if he does, the wine will burst the skins, and the wine is lost, and so are the skins; but new wine is for fresh skins (Mark 2:21–2).

The moment has come to establish the kingdom of God and for the coming kingdom it is no longer sufficient to adjust a commandment here, a tradition there. The renewal is radical and total. This does not mean that everything the Pharisees stood for would have to be abolished. As Jesus said in the Sermon on the Mount, in the Gospel of Matthew:

Think not that I have come to abolish the law and the prophets; I have not come to abolish them but to fulfil them (5:17).

In order to fulfil the Law and the prophets, it is not enough to fulfil all the commandments and obligations separately. On the contrary, the Law is a harmonious whole that covers all of life, and at its centre is the love for God and for one's neighbour. This is the meaning of another word by Jesus: 'till heaven and earth pass away, not an iota, not a dot will pass from the law until all is accomplished' (5:18). Every single element of the Law is important, but only in harmony with all the other commandments and with its centre, love. This is what many of the Pharisees could not accept. For that reason Jesus added a warning to his disciples and to us: I tell you, unless your righteousness is more plentiful than that of the scribes and Pharisees, you will never enter the kingdom of heaven' (5:20.) In this text I have departed from the Revised Standard Version, US edition, 1967: where the RSV has 'unless your righteousness exceeds that of the scribes and Pharisees', the Greek has a double comparative degree, is 'more plentiful than'). This, however, leads us to a final question. How did Jesus try to overcome the hostility of the Pharisees?' Did he indeed show that his *righteousness is more plentiful than that of the scribes and Pharisees*'?

5   In the Sermon on the Mount Jesus himself gives some advice on how to treat your enemies:

> I say to you, Love your enemies and pray for those who persecute you, so that you may be sons of your Father who is in heaven; for he makes his sun rise on the evil and on the good, and sends rain on the just and on the unjust. For if you love those who love you, what reward have you? Do not even the tax collectors do the same? And if you salute only your brethren, what more are you doing than others? Do not even the Gentiles do the same? You, therefore, must be perfect, as your heavenly Father is perfect (Matt. 5:44–8).

This is rather difficult to understand, let alone to practise: Jesus treated every person and every group in the same way; and if he treated some persons with even more consideration and love than others, than for instance

51

the Pharisees, it was because those people needed his attention more.

At the end of this meditation I am happy to say that some of the Pharisees did indeed understand the significance of what Jesus did and said. We even read in the Gospel of Luke that 'some Pharisees came, and said to him [Jesus], "Get away from here, for Herod wants to kill you"' (13:31). And later, after Jesus's death and resurrection, a number of Pharisees became Christians, most notably the apostle Paul.

There is no reason at all for enmity to continue between people and groups of people: between nations and between religions, between churches and between factions, between families and between individuals. It is possible to create a climate where there can be discussion and even confrontation without hostility or hatred. But this can only happen if we take Jesus's words in the Sermon on the Mount seriously. For the Pharisees the Law was the ideal; Jesus reversed this and proclaimed that the ideal was law. The ideal demands, as he tells us, that we must not only love our relatives and friends, but also the people who dislike us, and with whom we disagree. God loves the people who are opposed to him, who disobey him, who attempt to thwart his plans. He gives them every chance. In the same way we should be able to overcome hostility and even hatred, by always remembering Jesus's commandment: 'You, therefore, must be perfect, as your heavenly Father is perfect' (Matt. 5:48).

May I tell you a beautiful story? It is not from the Gospel, but from the heirs of the Pharisees, the rabbis. It is an illustration of a text from the book of Psalms (133:1), which Jesus will have said many times: 'Behold, how good and pleasant it is when brothers dwell in unity!'

Long before the temple was built in Jerusalem, there was on that location a field which was owned by a father and his two sons. They cultivated the land together, the three of them. When the father died, the sons decided that they would not divide the land, but go on cultivating the field together. One of the brothers had a wife and children, the other was not married. After the first harvest in the new situation they divided the yield. Each brought his share into his own barn. That night neither of them could sleep. The unmarried brother reproached himself that it was not right that he should receive the same as his brother, who had to provide for a whole family. So he decided to bring part of his share to the barn of his brother. During the same night the married brother reproached himself that it was not right that he should receive the same for himself and for his family, as his brother who was alone. For he would have nobody to provide for him when he became old. So he decided to bring part of his share to the barn of his brother. In between the two barns the two brothers met. Full of emotion they embraced each other. The Holy One – blessed be he – saw the togetherness of these brothers and said: the place where brothers are living together in such a way is where I want to live.

The temple no longer exists but together we are the house of God.

Brothers and Sisters, may the Holy Spirit enlighten our minds to see with Jesus the ideal as law for our way of life. May He help us to understand that we are completely dependent on grace. May He inspire us. Amen.

Cardinal Jean-Marie Lustiger

Archbishop of Paris

Aron Lustiger was born in Paris on 19 September 1926, of French Jewish parents who had both immigrated from Poland. He was educated at the Lycée Montaigne in Paris. During World War II he was baptised at his own request in Orléans and took Jean-Marie as his Christian name with the decision to become a priest.

However, he had to hide and work in a factory in Southern France. His mother was deported by the Nazis and died at Auschwitz. He joined the Christian resistance movement and helped found both the students' union and the Catholic chaplaincy at the Sorbonne before entering the Seminary of Paris. He was ordained in 1954 and served until 1959 as Assistant Chaplain to the students of the Sorbonne, then until 1969 as Chaplain of all Universities of Greater Paris. From 1969 to 1979 he was Pastor of the parish of Sainte Jeanne de Chantal in Paris. In 1979, he was appointed Bishop of Orléans, where he immediately opened a new Diocesan Seminary.

He was transferred back to Paris in 1981 to succeed Cardinal Francois Marty as Archbishop and was elevated to Cardinal in 1983. Cardinal Lustiger has since participated in several Roman Synods and co-presided at the 1991 European Synod. Some of his books published in English are: *Dare to Believe* and *Dare to Live* (Crossroads), *The Mass* (Harper & Row), *Dare to Rejoice* and *The Lord's Prayer* (Our Sunday Visitor), *First Steps in Prayer* (Harper-Collins), *Choosing God, Chosen by God* (Ignatius Press).

Cardinal Jean-Marie Lustiger
Archbishop of Paris

Jesus meets the lepers:
embracing the outcasts of society

(Matthew 8:1–4)

4

As Jesus was entering a village he was met by ten men with leprosy. They stood some way off and called out to him, 'Jesus, Master, take pity on us!'

That they should have to stand some way off, as St Luke reports in his Gospel (17:12–19), is no surprise to us: this is obviously for fear of the contagion, or because of the revulsion that they arouse. Anyway, what we have here is what today we call social exclusion, or marginalisation. These people are outcasts, or misfits, or derelicts, or pariahs, or untouchables, or exiles.

This is what we are tempted to call all those who are not like 'everyone' – all those who are not 'correct', whether politically, socially, psychologically, physically, economically, or whatever. The point is that in our culture all those who do not conform to the norms of the moment are thought to deserve pity.

From our point of view, what is most disgraceful about these ten men is not so much that they are *lepers*, but that their leprosy causes them to be *rejected*.

The Gospels virtually ignore the well-supplied lexicon, the rich vocabulary, that is being used these days to refer to social exclusion. But they do point out quite accurately the ills and the pains which overwhelm human beings and from which Jesus delivers them.

There are all the *diseases* that Jesus is asked to cure: infirmities (ἄρρωστος), blindness, muteness, paralysis, insanity, all kinds of illnesses. And people suffering

57

from various sicknesses (μάστιξ), such as torments (βασαυος), listlessness (μαλακία), or weakness (ἀσθένεια), come to him as well.

There is also *leprosy*. As a matter of fact, it is not a disease. Jesus does not cure the lepers: he cleanses them.

Then there is *possession*. But again, when someone is suffering because he is possessed by an evil spirit, Jesus does not heal him: he simply drives the demon away.

In addition, there is *sin*. and this is even more amazing: Jesus forgives sins. If the paralysed man of Capernaum can walk away, it seems to be a mere extra (Luke 5:17–26).

And finally there is *death*; Jesus raises the dead.

By acting so efficiently, Jesus 'shows the glad tidings of the kingdom of God' (Luke 8:1). This is the good news of salvation – the Gospel he proclaims.

So when John from his prison sends some of his disciples to ask Jesus, 'Are you the one who is to come?', that is to say, 'Are you the Messiah?', Jesus answers (Matt.11:2–6), 'Go and report to John what you hear and see: the blind recover sight, the lame walk, lepers are made clean, the deaf hear, the dead are raised to life, the poor are brought good news. Blessed are those who do not find me an obstacle to faith.'

So what we have to strive to understand is why Jesus gives the cleansing of the lepers as a messianic sign of the advent of the kingdom of God.

The visible symptoms of leprosy – with the disfigured, eaten-up face – practically usher a person who is still alive into the realm of death. The progress of the condition reminds us of the decay of a corpse. This is why Leviticus (ch. 13–14) speaks of leprosy as the exemplary 'plague' – in Hebrew *nega* – with which God 'strikes' – in Hebrew *naga* – the sinners. The leper appears as a living dead man.

Leprosy symbolises the separation from God. It is the sign of sin. It makes visible the death which sin entails. In this respect, leprosy epitomises utter defilement.

In the Bible, as in the ancient Semitic religions, the notions of purity and impurity are linked to death and therefore to sin. For God is the source of life. He gives life. So when man turns away from God, when he fails to follow God's Law of life, he consorts with death and is doomed to die. Only God can purify him and give him life.

This is why Leviticus 14 requests the priest, after he has examined the leper and acknowledged that God has cleansed him, to perform the sacrifices of purification-offering, then the sacrifice of reparation-offering and the expiation rite for uncleanness. Finally, the priest shall slaughter the whole-offering and present it along with the grain-offering on the altar.

This allows us to understand the dismay of the king of Israel, when he receives the visit of Naaman, commander of the king of Aram's army, carrying a letter from his master, which reads: 'This letter is to inform you that I am sending to you my servant Naaman so that you may cure him of his leprosy.' The king of Israel is frightened because he knows that God alone can carry out such a feat. So he tears his clothes and says, 'Am I God to kill and make alive, that this fellow should send me a man to cure him of his disease?' But Elisha comforts the king of Israel by saying to him, 'Let Naaman come to me, and he will know that there is a prophet in Israel' (2 Kings 5:1–19).

What is meant by 'prophet' is a man through whom God acts and speaks.

It should then come as no surprise to us to see how accurately the three synoptic Gospels report, among the first signs given by Jesus, the healing of a leper. The theme of this meditation is seen in Matthew 8:1–4. There are parallels in Mark 1:40–4 and Luke 5:12–14.

The narratives of this cleansing have a definitely liturgical ring. St Matthew tells us that the leper bows before Jesus. St Mark says that he kneels down. St Luke has him throw himself to the ground. He even makes the prostration more explicitly liturgical by adding that the man *beseeches* Jesus for help.

The leper's prayer is no less characteristic. He first calls Jesus 'Lord' (Κύριε). Also, he begs for mercy: 'If you will, you can . . .' And he does not ask to be healed, but to be purified: 'If you will, you can cleanse me.' When we hear this, we ought to wonder: who else than God can purify from leprosy? Just as the people of Capernaum wonder a little later, 'Who but God alone can forgive sins?' (Luke 5:21).

Jesus's response is even more amazing: he 'stretched out his hand and touched him, saying, "I will; be clean."'

Purification coincides with what Jesus says and does. As the leper has guessed, Jesus possesses a strength, the divine power to free him, just as he has the divine power to forgive sins on earth, whereas the priests of the temple can only acknowledge the healing by offering the sacrifice for the purification from sin.

It would be a mistake to think that when Jesus touches the leper he is challenging a taboo, or that this brush of the hand risks making him impure in his turn. Through this physical contact Jesus gives a sign that his body cures evils, because 'his flesh never saw corruption'. This is what St Peter says in his first speech on Whit Sunday when he announces the resurrection of Jesus (Acts 2:27,31; see Psalm 16:10). And the evangelists do not fail to underline that the body of Jesus is – as much as his words – the source of life.

The cleansed leper already partakes in Christ's living

body. With this gesture, Jesus gives us to grasp the ecclesial dimension of salvation. This dimension is clearly perceptible in the evangelists' testimonies. The realism of the Synoptic Gospels thus prevents us from reducing the phrase 'the body of Christ', as St Paul uses it in 1 Corinthians 12:12, to a simple metaphor. The same body of Christ, born from the Virgin Mary, given as food, crucified and glorified, is the source of life – for the leper as it is for the Christian whom baptism in the Church has made a member of this Body.

Jesus then instructs the leper not to tell anyone. If we want fully to understand this prohibition, we must not limit ourselves to considering the so-called 'messianic secret' as a pedagogic precaution. In the Gospels' narratives, the glory of Jesus is still veiled and is to be revealed at his resurrection.

After this, Jesus tells the leper, 'Go, show yourself to the priest and make the offering laid down by Moses for your cleansing: that will be a sign for them.' The final comment may take us aback. 'Them' cannot but mean the priests of the temple. However, the question is: how can a cleansed leper showing up to ask for the rites and sacrifices ordered by Moses become a sign for the priests?

Such a purification proves that there lives in Israel, as in the time of Elisha. a prophet – and a great prophet. The point is that Jesus himself, as St Luke reports (4:24–7), has, at the synagogue of Nazareth, just explained the meaning of the cleansing of Naaman the Syrian. Consequently, the priests will have to ask themselves a disturbing question about such an extraordinary divine intervention: *who* is this prophet whom God has thus sent?

In fact, everything in this amazingly liturgical narrative allows us to guess that the priestly mystery of the temple has somehow materialised in the person of Jesus. A few verses farther on from our theme passage, in his testimony

(8:16–17) Matthew emphasises Jesus's messianic accomplishment and quotes the fourth poem of the Suffering Servant (Isa. 53:4): 'To fulfil the prophecy of Isaiah, "He took our illnesses and carried our sicknesses."' The Suffering Servant is compared to a leper: 'His form has lost all human likeness' (Isa. 52:14); he is disfigured by the burden of the sin and death that he is taking up to deliver us.

One more observation is to be made about the healing of the ten lepers which I recalled at the beginning of this meditation and which St Luke alone reports.

As far as these ten men are concerned, Jesus sends them to show themselves only to the priest. They are cleansed as they are on their way. Yet only one of them comes back to glorify God: 'He threw himself at Jesus's feet and gave him thanks.'

He is a Samaritan – an alien. He will be the only one to whom Jesus will be able to say. 'Stand up and go on your way; your faith has cured you.'

This leper is the prophetic sign of the universal salvation that had been promised by the prophets. This is what Jesus has already announced at the synagogue of Nazareth: 'In the time of the prophet Elisha there were many lepers in Israel, and not one of them was healed, but only Naaman, the Syrian.' (Luke 4:27).

As for Jesus's questions, 'Were not all ten men made clean? The other nine, where are they?', we may hear them addressed to the thanklessness of all ungrateful Christians – those who have been baptised in Christ and thus 'are no longer aliens', as St Paul puts it in his epistle to the Ephesians (2:19), but partake in Christ's life, and yet have become forgetful of the grace they have received.

We now have to conclude and draw the consequences of what we have found in the Gospel.

Today's doctors know how to cure leprosy and hope to deliver humankind from it. Nowadays, the nature of this terrible affliction is clearly known and proves to be comparable to many others. Shall we then consider the specific significance of leprosy in the Bible as one more piece of now archaic, obsolete, useless information? It would certainly be better to recognise in the sorry condition of lepers in ancient times a foreboding of present-day exclusion.

Either alternative would amount to imposing an external significance on the biblical symbolism, however, instead of exploring the relevance of its message in our lives.

In the first place, as we have noted, leprosy is seen in the Bible as the invasion of death among the living. It is the visible face of the sin by which man turns away from God, who is the source of life.

What stigmata of death can be detected at the end of this millennium? Unfortunately it is only too easy to make a list and thus run the risk of sounding unduly pessimistic: wars, massacres, injustices, tortures, famines, contempt of human life from its inception to its termination, drugs, homelessness, poverty . . . It is less easy to wonder why such a brilliant civilisation as ours consorts with death so assiduously. Why do so many suicidal or murderous impulses emerge?

The divine Word presents a deeper, less naïve vision of the human condition. The Word of God summons us to make out, under the mask of death, the sin that leads to it. The Word also urges us to crave for and love the life whose source is in God. This is how we may find the cure that can actually deliver us from the fascination of death. This is how we may discover the actual magnitude of the struggle in which humankind is involved.

In the second place, when Jesus cleanses the leper, he fully, totally gives life to this man.

When today Jesus, through his Church, says to those who beseech him, 'I will; be clean', he gives them God's forgiveness, and they are fully, totally cured from their sins. It is 'for them a new creation', as the Scriptures say (2 Cor. 5:17; Gal. 5:13; see Isa. 65:17ff).

Our faith remains paralysed by our fear and our acquiescence to being the slaves of our own selves. Jesus often asks those who call upon him. 'What do you want me to do for you?' What do *you* want? We are often incapable of *wanting* to be healed, cleansed, forgiven. As children of the end of this century, we keep on dreaming of miraculous improvements in human potentials, while irresistibly resigning ourselves to anticipate the worst. It is precisely from this resignation to sin that Jesus wants to purify us. All we have to do is to allow ourselves to be transformed by the divine power of his forgiveness.

Shall we, like the nine ungrateful lepers, forget the power of life? Shall we forget the salvation that the suffering and resurrected Messiah is bringing into this world? Are we going to evade the mission we are entrusted with, to bear witness to the hope that is born in the conscience of the man who has been restored to life?

The cleansing of the lepers expresses God's will to give back to man, through his Son, his true face of a child of God. Amen!

Cardinal Godfried Danneels

Archbishop of Malines-Brussels

Godfried Danneels was born in Kanegem (province of West Flanders) in 1933. He studied at the Leo XIII College of the Catholic University of Louvain and graduated with a master's degree in philosophy. He was sent to the Belgian College in Rome, was ordained priest in 1957 and obtained his DD at the Gregorian University in Rome in 1961. In 1977 he was appointed Bishop of Antwerp and in 1978 was appointed a member of the Roman Congregation of the Doctrine of the Faith for five years.

In 1979 Pope John Paul appointed him as second delegate chairman together with Cardinal J. Willebrands at the special Synod of Dutch Bishops held in Rome in 1980.

In December 1979 Pope John Paul appointed Mgr. Godfried Danneels as Archbishop of Malines-Brussels, succeeding Cardinal Suenens who resigned when attaining the age limit of 75 years. According to the statutes of the Church of Belgium, he also became Chairman of the Conference of Belgian Bishops. He was canonically enthroned in the Cathedral of Malines on January 4, 1980.

Later that year he was appointed Ordinary of the Armed Forces of Belgium, and he represented the Bishops' Conference of Belgium at the synod held in Rome in 1980 and in 1983. In between he was elected as one of the permanent Sacretariat of the Synod of Bishops.

In 1985 he was named Relator of the special Synod of Bishops, at the occasioin of the 20th anniversary of the Second Vatican Council and in 1987 was appointed as member of the Special Synod of Dutch Bishops.

Since 1990 he has been International president of Pax Christi.

Cardinal Godfried Danneels
Archbishop of Malines-Brussels

Jesus meets the Samaritan woman:
touching a society in search of God

(John 4:1–42)

5

God in Search of People –
People in Search of God

The Gospel passage of Jesus's encounter with the Samaritan woman is at the centre of both the Gospel of John and the Lenten liturgy. Together with the stories of the man born blind and the raising of Lazarus, it also belongs to the basic instruction of baptismal candidates. Living water (John 4), the light of faith (John 9), and eternal life (John 11) are mentioned. These are all baptismal themes. But they also depict the path of the candidates on the road to faith and to the sacrament of Baptism.

My theme is Jesus's meeting with the Samaritan woman, a meeting between the Saviour and the woman, between God and the people, between the Church and the world.

The World in Search of God

It is not coincidental that the meeting takes place at the well of Jacob of Sychar, at the foot of Mount Garizim. All this evokes the charm of the time of the Patriarchs. They travelled from well to well, with family and livestock, in search of life. Water was life, and thirst was death. At each oasis the cry of joy found in the Book of Numbers could be heard: 'Spring up, O well! Sing to it! the well which the princes dug, which the nobles of the people delved, with the sceptre and with their staves' (Num. 21:17).

The Patriarchs travelled from spring to spring. It was there that all meetings occurred: that of Abraham and Rebecca (Gen. 24:15), that of Jacob and Rachel (Gen. 29:1–14), that of Moses and the daughters of Reuel (Exod. 2:16). Where there was water, there was life and conviviality. Where there is water, God is there. The charm of the wells runs throughout the entire Bible.

The whole world is in search of God. Has there ever been a time when people sought with more intensity than they do today for something that goes beyond science, technology, and comfort? Often these searches take strange forms: sects and occult societies, New Age, all kinds of techniques which relax and expand consciousness. Our time of wild religiosity is not a time without God. It is rather a time of many gods. The whole world is in search of God, by other noble names like peace, justice, harmony, wisdom, renewal and universal brother-and-sisterhood. Our times are in search of God.

God is Already There . . .

Even if people look for wells to find God, God is even more in search of people. According to the legend of the well, the source of water, who was Christ, accompanied the people of Israel on all their journeys through the desert. They themselves said that it was this well which paused at Sychar for Jacob, and there continued to bring forth water. Long before the world sought God, God sought the world. People do not create water: all springs come forth from the Garden of Eden with which God irrigated the entire world. If it is true that our civilisation is in search of God, it is even more true that God is in search of our civilisation and culture. Before we even arrive, he is already there. So Jesus is already there at Jacob's well when the woman arrives. He just sits, tired from the journey, and he waits.

There is still more: It is Jesus who speaks first: 'Give me a drink . . .' This is the great paradox. We think that we enquire about God. No, he enquires about us. We need God, but God seems to need us. We thirst after God, but God thirsts even more after us. We are in search of a strong God, we find a weak Messiah, dead from thirst, whom we then must help.

God allows himself to be known as a needy person. He says to our world and to our culture: 'I need you.' In this way he wants to show us how he needs us, how important we are to him. Then we shall recognise how important he is for us. God is (in the first place) the beggar, we the generous givers. Was this not the only manner for God to gain our confidence? The giver must disguise himself as a beggar.

So God says to our entire culture: 'Give me a drink.' Until we see that, under the rags of the beggar, there is a rich man from whom we can expect everything.

If You Knew the Gift of God

The woman is in search of Water. She is in search of a way to avoid the daily task of having to carry the jar on her head from the village to the well in the heat of the noonday sun.

But the real water seems to be different from that of which the woman is thinking. What Jesus wants to give her is water and yet not water. It is 'living' water, that is water from the bottom of the well which you cannot reach with a bucket. But it also a different kind of water: water which springs forth to eternal life. Like Nicodemus in the night, Jesus changes registers and speaks another language. Jesus wants to raise Nicodemus and the Samaritan woman to a different level: he speaks with different words, with another grammar. He speaks the language of faith. This language is connected with the language of the world, but also transcends it. 'Being born' is here no longer to come from the womb of the mother, but to be born from water and the Holy Spirit; drinking no longer quenches material thirst, but a spiritual thirst for happiness.

It is the same in our culture: our desires are not satisfied but raised up and spiritualised. Words mean something different and something more: justice means not only correct relations between people but correct relations with God; peace is not only silencing weapons, but Messianic *shalom*, universal harmony between heaven and earth, established on the cross; life is not only life here and now, but eternal life beyond death; water is not only water to wash the body, but the water of baptism; eating is not only feeding oneself in order to live, but eating in order to gain eternal life.

The first and main obstacle in the search of our culture for God is precisely this leap of faith to this new language which comes from somewhere else: the analogical language of faith, which seems to refer to things here, everyday things, but actually refers to the things of God. If you knew the gift of God you would ask for water, says Jesus. If our culture is to find God, it must find the power and the grace not to depreciate purely technological-scientific thinking, but to break through it. It must find the power and the grace to tear the curtain in front of the temple and to penetrate to the depths of things and of language. We need to heal language: it was made to say things which cannot be explained.

Our culture suffers from a blind spot on the retina. What Guardini called the impotence of contemplation, of looking into the heart of things. The reduction of our knowledge to its purely quantifiable aspect is the greatest visual handicap of our time. Not that pure scientific knowledge is wrong, but rather its monopoly and its exclusivity is wrong. There are invisible things in the universe which must be approached with different ways of knowing. The despair in the omnipotence of science and technology increases in our time, but the risk is that the alternative will not be faith but superstition and irrationality.

Moral impotence

The dialogue between Jesus and the Samaritan woman doesn't stop: the woman asks for such living water, although she doesn't know what it means. But she is open to every surprise. Openness is essential: she is openness and thus she is the gate to faith. The woman is prepared to climb from the ground floor of empirical evidence to the first floor of giving oneself over to faith. But is she able to reach that far?

For her there is another obstacle: that of moral impotence. 'Go, call your husband,' says Jesus. She says she has none. It seems she has already had five and that the sixth is not even her husband. She is not lying, but she also doesn't confess her evil. She avoids. The second obstacle for each human being and for our times and culture is the moral impotence in which we are imprisoned. One cannot know God and cannot find nor accept the Messiah if the heaviness of sin weighs on one's heart. Immorality troubles the view as much as the blind spot of unbelief. One who wants to believe must, like Abraham, be able to leave their land, with the certainty of natural evidences and the burden of sin.

But what is the sin of our time, what is contemporary moral impotence? Certainly, the sins of our time are also the sins of all time: they concern the same commandments and the same trespasses. The hearts of people have remained the same, yet the means which the evil heart has at its disposal are greater and more dangerous. Our wars are more deadly than those of our fathers. Those who wage them are thus also more guilty and more sinful.

But the sin of our times has its own shape. Which shape? Is it not the perversion of the truth rather than the perversion of the heart? Perhaps the sinfulness of our time is precisely that that sinfulness is denied, rejected, neutralised, or declared neurotic. Is this not the basic point of 'Veritatis Splendor'?

The content of morality is not questioned, but the foundations themselves of morality are doubted. The question is not so much what is good or evil, but do good and evil still exist? One no longer asks about what natural law says, but is there evil which is always evil? The question is not so much what does God say, but does God have anything to say or do we create morality and determine good and evil ourselves? The building itself is threatened, no longer only the decorations.

What would happen if one no longer considered abortion as morally reprehensible but as a human right? This is no longer a weakness of the heart but the perversion of thinking. The disease of our culture and its obscuring of God are embedded in thinking more than in doing.

This perversion of thinking consists also in the secularisation of values, in their cutting off from their transcendental source, which is God. It probably also explains the lack of joy and the melancholy of our culture. Happiness is gone. Is this joylessness, although, no doubt unconscious, not related to the obscuring of God, or the absence of God: the absence especially of a forgiving nature, of a merciful God? However much feelings of guilt might be neutralised by perverted thinking, the heart cannot be comforted by the illusory myth of innocence. Where there is no longer a God forgiving of moral impotence, people die.

Once there lived a king and a servant. The king proclaimed his laws and the servant said: 'I will follow them.' But each evening he realised that, in spite of his good will and his efforts, he had broken the law. Every evening he went to the king and asked for and received forgiveness. This happened every day. One day the king died. No one ever knew whether it was a natural death or whether the king was murdered. But he was no longer there. Now the servant could no longer ask for forgiveness, which was difficult. He said, 'I cannot go on living like this. Something must be done.' But what? So he said to himself: 'I shall dispense with the law. Then there will no longer be any lawbreaking, any feeling of guilt. Then I shall no longer have to ask forgiveness. I can easily do without the king.'

So this was done; he dispensed with the law and said: 'From now on there are no longer good and evil.' But every evening the feeling of guilt returned. It remained difficult even though there were no longer any law and no longer any evil. The servant found neither rest nor joy and realised that this state of affairs could also no longer continue. 'Perhaps dispensing with the law was my greatest evil,' he thought. Eventually he sought the advice of a wise person and told of his problems. Then the wise person said: 'There is only one way out, my friend. The king must be resurrected.'

Is not this moral impotence at the root of our culture? God is gone – some have killed him, others no longer need him, but there is no longer anyone who can forgive, and dispensing with the law and calling evil 'good' offer no comfort.

'Go call your husband,' says Jesus. We had better not answer: 'Lord, I have no husband; I wouldn't know where I fall short.' The second obstacle to the search for God is this perversion of thinking and the myth of innocence. The absence of God creates another obstacle in our culture and narcissistic tendencies.

The Religious Market-place

Then the dialogue between Jesus and the woman takes another turn. The woman is afraid of the personal nature of the interrogation. The prophetic language escapes her; she quickly switches from the I-form to the we-form, and from the personal interrogation to a curiosity question about unimportant 'religious questions'. 'Our fathers worshipped on this mountain; and you say that in Jerusalem is the place men ought to worship.' Jesus avoids the question and says: 'Woman, this is not the issue.' The invitation to personal conversion is twisted by the woman into a noncommittal question for information. The personalisation of the dialogue gets bogged down in a piece of information. Now 'I' is no longer the subject of the sentence, but an impersonal 'we'.

The woman goes the way of the religious market-place. Our times often do this too; with each personal interrogation we shield ourselves and divert the discussion to unimportant ecclesial and extra-ecclesial topics. This is the third obstacle in the search for God: the reduction of the problem of 'shall I repent?' to a visit to the religious supermarket, which nowadays is well stocked. I escape the impasse of the personal question of God to me: 'Turn back to me and I will turn towards you', and proceed to the noncommittal abundance of the religious supermarket. The problem is not 'what should I do?' but 'what is available in the market-place?'

Our society buzzes with religious questions and the answers are numerous. Many of these present themselves as therapies for the pain of the contemporary person: they want to heal. The most famous of this sort is undoubtedly New Age, a nebulous collection of conceptions and techniques with the goal of freeing the person from the triple pain of poverty, stress, and disharmony. Not everything in this field is wrong: there are comforting ideas and relaxation techniques.

But what is conspicuous is that almost nowhere is there talk of personal conversion and of the integration of suffering and the Cross in the recommended salvation therapy. Often a path to happiness is sketched which is 'soft' and which excludes personal commitment and the dying to self-centredness. The question here is, of course, whether the effort towards moral turnabout can be replaced by a sort of spiritual knowledge. The question is: can a so-called higher knowledge alone, a new gnosis, a mere 'enlightenment', really save? Too many people today think that knowledge alone can save. Not only must our understandings see, but our hearts must be moved towards a deeper energy than light alone. Strength is also necessary. Jesus is not merely a teacher, a source of knowledge and the solution to our religious curiosity. Jesus is also Saviour. He opens our eyes, but also much more: he moves our hearts.

We have heard Him Ourselves

Jesus goes into the town of Sychar. The woman has already told the inhabitants everything: 'He told me all that I ever did,' she said. But later the inhabitants of Sychar say: 'It is no longer because of your words that we believe, for we

have heard for ourselves, and we know that this is indeed
the Saviour of the world' (John 4:42).

In our times there is only one way to find God and his
Christ: the world itself must hear him. His word is the
only thing that can give living water. We must hear him
ourselves.

Also, the three obstacles which in our culture separate
us from him can only be overcome in this same way. What
else besides his Word could raise us from the level of
shallow evidence to the level of faith? Only the docility of
hearing – *fides ex auditu* – can arouse faith in ourselves.
And we know that he is is like rain from heaven. He falls
to the earth and doesn't return without giving the earth its
fertility.

But moral impotence and sin cannot be overcome
except through the power of his Word: his Word alone
can convert us.

Likewise his Word and his Word alone can point us to
where the true sources of happiness lie in the religious
supermarket of today. Christ's Word says that there is no
cheap or quick or automatic method of becoming happy, of
being saved. Enlightenment does not save, only conversion
saves. An easy way to God does not exist: you cannot
eliminate the Cross.

We believe too little in the power of his Word. Without
giving a magic meaning to bare proclamation, it is the
case that his Word – correctly and purely proclaimed in
grace, is irresistible and powerful. It presents it fruits and
does not return empty handed. It is condensed into the
Sacraments, which are the 'strong words' of the Church. In
the fourth chapter of Mark, Jesus elucidates in parables the
irresistible power of the Word. The seed of the Word finds
its way. There will always be rocky soil, well-worn paths,
thistles and thorns, and shallow soil. The seed carries its
fruit somewhere: thirty-, sixty-, and one hundred-fold. It

bears fruits from its own seed, so the farmer may sleep restfully. And the Word is so powerful that it grows disproportionately: the smallest seed becomes the largest tree in which all the birds can nest.

Cardinal George Basil Hume, OSB

Archbishop of Westminster

George Basil Hume was born in 1923 in Newcastle upon Tyne. He was educated at Ampleforth College and in 1941 he entered the Monastery at Ampleforth and in the following years pursued academic studies at Oxford and Freiburg Universities.

He was ordained priest in 1950 and for the following twelve years taught modern languages at Ampleforth College.

In 1963 he was elected Abbot of Ampleforth. He held this post until 1976 when he was appointed Archbishop of Westminster by Pope Paul VI. In the same year he was appointed Cardinal-priest with the title of San Silvestro in Capite. Cardinal Hume has been President of the Bishops' Conference of England and Wales since 1979 and was also President of the Council of European Bishops' Conferences between 1979 and 1987.

One of the most outstanding events to have occurred to date during his time as Cardinal is the visit of Pope John Paul II to Britain in May 1982. The visit proved to be tremendously successful. It fostered closer ecumenical relations, which is an element still high on the Cardinal's list of priorities.

Cardinal Hume has shown great concern for human rights and injustice and in particular has been involved in the cases of the Guildford Four and the Maguires. He has given a priority to education in his diocese and remains actively involved in the debate over educational reform.

He has published several books, the most recent in 1994 titled *Remarking Europe: the Gospel in a divided Continent*.

Cardinal George Basil Hume, OSB
Archbishop of Westminster

Jesus meets Martha and Mary:
finding time for God in a busy life

(Luke 10:38–41; John 11:1–7, 17–27; 12:1–8)

6

We lived at No. 4; they lived at No. 11. We, the five youngest members of our family, were not yet in our teens; they, three ladies and their brother, were already elderly, or at least seemed so to us. We used to visit them, and they us. They were kind, hospitable, generous, welcoming. When we arrived we sensed that they had no other concern but us. We liked to visit them. Then one day the brother died and his sisters mourned him, and so did we. His name was Frank. Why had he died? Where had he gone? Encounter with death at an early age makes the young ask grown-up questions. We did. And the sisters? They were sad, very sad. If only . . . if only . . . why him? Why now? Such thoughts, and the sadness that is their companion, are part of every family's story.

It happened to two sisters in Our Lord's time, Martha and Mary, when their brother Lazarus died. They mourned. They were sad. 'If only . . . if you had been here, Lord, my brother would not have died.' Martha said that. There was always a peremptory note in her voice, even a rebuking one, when Martha spoke.

Jesus's relationship to the two sisters and their brother was very close. 'Jesus loved Martha and her sister and Lazarus.' One day the sisters had to send an urgent message to Jesus. Lazarus was sick. 'Lord, the man you love is ill,' they said. Then Lazarus died. Jesus was sad. He wept. But he did intervene. He restored Lazarus to life.

How often Jesus visited these friends we do not know. Certainly just before his terrible death, six days in fact, he went to their home in Bethany. Lazarus was there, too. That visit was the occasion when Mary got carried away. Well, some would say 'carried away', too enthusiastic perhaps. She anointed Jesus with a pound of costly ointment, pure nard, and with it anointed the feet of Jesus too, wiping them with her hair. Over the top? Maybe. Judas thought so: 'Why was this ointment not sold for three hundred denarii and the money given to the poor?' But Judas was not being honest. 'He said this not because he cared about the poor, but because he was a thief.' Judas had spoken to Jesus, but as hypocrites do.

There was another occasion when Jesus visited the two sisters. Martha, again with a slight edge to her voice, reacted characteristically to what she felt was the wrong being done to her by her sister. Here she was hard at work preparing the meal while Mary sat at Jesus's feet doing nothing. 'Doing nothing'? – hardly. Jesus defended Mary and said to Martha, 'Mary has chosen the better part and it is not to be taken from her' (v. 42).

There was indeed a close friendship between Jesus and Mary, and with her brother and sister.

Let us look more closely at this friendship. 'Jesus loved Martha and her sister and Lazarus', we have read. That love was indeed a human love. Jesus had a human heart, an affectionate nature. He had emotions like ours, but they never ran wild or out of control, as sometimes is the case with us. Jesus knew the joys of human love and its pains. He loved Judas, but Judas was to betray him. That hurt. Yes, Jesus loved in a human way. Indeed no one loved more perfectly in a human way than he. He, and none better than he, knew how to love as a friend. There was, however, more to Jesus's loving. Jesus was both God and man. The loving was human, but the lover was God. The love he gave channelled, as it were, the divine love which was his too.

When we seek to explore the meaning of love in God, we have no starting-point other than our own experience of loving. Our experience can help us to understand what John, the apostle, meant when he wrote: 'God is Love' (1 John 4:8). Love was a reality in God before it ever became an experience between humans. It has been well said that the language of love belongs by right to God first rather than to us. Humans only borrow it. If we want to know what love truly is, then we shall not do so until we see God in vision. Then we shall see love in all its beauty and truth. God is the origin of love in all its different forms and expressions. Human love reflects divine love and, indeed, transmits it. The love of a parent, for example, speaks of the love which God has for the children of those parents. That is why children who have never known the love of a parent cannot know what the word 'love' means when applied to God, or only with difficulty. Deprived of love in our lives we are never quite at ease in our relationships with God.

Why am I pursuing this point? It is because a healthy spiritual life must be based on a strong conviction that God's love for each of us is unconditional and total. It is a love that is strong, warm, intimate. Many people, perhaps too many, base their spiritual lives on fear. They do not necessarily admit to this, but it is so. There is, of course, a healthy fear of God that is part of our loving of him, but there is a neurotic fear that is destructive and saps spiritual energy. An authentic spirituality begins when we become convinced of God's love for us, when we realise that we are never rejected by him, when we know that we are wanted.

These, then, are some thoughts to guide our further reflection on Mary sitting at Jesus's feet and on Martha busying herself in the service of other people. Both in their different ways were responding to a love which Jesus had for each one. Both have something to teach us about prayer.

Let me speak first about Mary. Mary rejoiced in Jesus's company and he in hers. Friends must enjoy being with each other. Jesus and Mary had grown close. He enjoyed her company and she his. Such friendships need space to develop and grow strong. Friends must waste time together.

It is also thus in prayer. Prayer is making friends with God, and He with us. Prayer is trying to focus the mind on God, and trying to admit him into our hearts. Prayer is wasting time with God. Prayer needs space to develop and grow strong.

In Mary's relationship with Jesus there are important points to notice. They have a bearing on our prayer-lives. First, when Mary sat at Jesus's feet and looked at him she saw the man who was her friend, the one she loved. Did she have any idea, even then, that there was something more to be known about him? Did she sense, and because he had shown it to her as a special favour, that he was a son of God, or more accurately, the Son of God? We do not know. She may well have seen one thing and her faith told her another. Martha certainly seems to have instinctively recognised that Jesus was more than just a family friend, the welcome visitor to their home. She once spoke with great conviction. The occasion was Jesus's visit when Lazarus had died. Martha made a fine profession of faith, very similar to Peter's, when she said: 'Yes, Lord; I believe that you are the Christ, the Son of God, he who is coming into the world' (John 11:27). Mary, I think, would have said the same thing. For us it is clear. When we approach Christ in prayer or read about him in the Gospel, we know that it is to God that we are turning our thoughts or addressing our words. The man we meet in the Gospels is the God whom we are seeking.

Second, Jesus speaks to us of the Father. He reveals him. 'He who sees me sees the Father', Jesus had told Philip. To have seen Jesus, to have heard his voice was to have experienced in a human way something of God. How else could we learn about God save through human thoughts and words. We have no other, unless, of course, we were to find ourselves standing, as it were, on tip-toe to reach beyond ourselves and all that we know, into another world . . . but I cannot speak of that for it is the mystic's highest experience. It is a rare gift. St Paul had it, and several saints as well. But mystical experience is not the measure of sanctity. Doing God's will is. For most of us we must reach out to God in a more prosaic manner. A prayerful study of the man we meet in the Gospel is an important part of it.

Prayer has to be learned. For most of us it does not come naturally. We have to work at it. Now we learn to pray chiefly by praying, and experience tells us that the way we find easiest to pray is the best way for us. We cannot expect to achieve intimacy in our relationship with God at once. At first we may be like strangers. Our first attempts to pray seriously (rather than just saying prayers in a routine unthinking manner) may be awkward, hesitant, clumsy even. We do not know how to start, what to say. We have to learn. We start by treating God as an acquaintance before achieving that friendship which He wants to establish with us. We have probably from time to time tried to make contact with him, especially in times of crisis or when we have been badly in need of something; no harm in that, of course. Such prayers are important, but they do not lead necessarily to friendship with God. Again, so often when we pray we can so easily remain 'outside the words' we speak. We are not at one with the words we say. They do not express what we feel within ourselves or we do not make our own the thoughts the words convey. We find that we do not attend to the person whom we are supposed to be addressing. We speak almost casually to God, as if to an acquaintance and not to a friend.

How then should we proceed to develop a life of prayer? To do so we need to organise ourselves: we have to find space in the day when we, like Mary, can spend time trying to be in the presence of Jesus. I used the word 'trying'. In prayer it is the key concept. Our part is to 'try' to raise minds and hearts to God. When the 'trying' becomes effortless, indeed even sweet, we have received a gift. It is a gift for those who persevere, for those in need of encouragement, but strong souls are often asked just to go on 'trying' to raise minds and hearts to God day by day, waiting, wanting, but content to be shown no special favour.

How then should we proceed? One way would be to take words from a well-known prayer like the Lord's Prayer. Say it slowly, dwelling on each phrase or word, like a bee moving from flower to flower to collect the nectar it seeks. There may come a moment, when you do not want to move on to the next word, but wish just to pause and rest. A word or phrase may speak to you, give up its inner meaning or enable you even to enjoy a rare moment when you sense the presence of God. This is God speaking, his way of doing so, and from being the speaker you have become the listener, sitting at his feet like Mary. If that moment of peace and well-being occurs, then, as I have already said, that is a gift from God.

Another starting point in prayer can be to take a passage from the Gospel, a parable, perhaps, or a dialogue between Jesus and another person, with whom I can identify. Reading and reflecting, either alone or with others, on passages from the Gospel lead to our focusing our minds on Christ, his words and actions. It is the discovering of a friend. It is the beginning of prayer. Do not forget that the

Gospels speak today to everyone without exception. The words of Jesus are contemporary in every age.

Read the text slowly, knowing that he about whom we read is God who became man, and what we read is a personal message for you from God. This way of praying is a waiting and watching manner of proceeding. It may not be immediately or even often, that this Word of God will speak deep within us, leaving us with a sense that we have indeed been touched by God. That 'sense' is a gift, and from the Holy Spirit, who should always be called upon to give us his help whenever we begin our prayer.

Quite often – perhaps even very often – our praying words slowly, or reflecting on a Gospel passage may seem to be frustrating and unrewarding. Do not be surprised or anxious. Such a situation purifies our motive for praying which is primarily to please God, not to comfort ourselves. Our perseverance is, too, a proof of our love.

Jesus visited Martha and Mary on more than one occasion. He knocked often at their door, and was received. I should imagine that from time to time one or other of the two women was less than on top form. They would not be human if they never experienced changes of mood or were never burdened with anxieties and worries. Maybe sometimes Mary would have found no joy in sitting and listening, perhaps at other times so burdened that fine thoughts and words were of no help. I think of her sitting, anguished, upset but pleased, none the less, just to be with Jesus. She knew that he understood. After all he had himself known darkness, and later on would suffer greatly. So abandoned by God did he feel that he could only express himself through praying a psalm: 'My God, my God, why hast thou forsaken me?'

You are anguished, burdened, in pain? You are mourning a loved one, angry because of some injustice, betrayed by a friend, or just worn out and jaded? Such experiences

87

dull the mind, rob it of peace and serenity, leave us exhausted and depressed. 'Don't ask me to speak to God. Words are useless. I cannot think straight,' I hear you say. It is then that you should hear him call, 'Come to me all you who labour and are heavy-laden and I will give you rest' (Matt. 11:28). Your prayer will be simple, but not easy. It is just to be in his presence, sitting at his feet, no thoughts, no words, watching, waiting for him to heal the pain or at least to soften it. Our pain is his, and he calls us to join him in his: 'Take my yoke upon you, and learn from me; for I am gentle and lowly in heart, and you will find rest for your souls' (v. 29).

There is no finer prayer when the yoke truly weighs upon us than to say with him: 'Father, if you are willing, remove this cup from me, but not my will, but yours be done' (Luke 22:42), or one of the last words he spoke, again from a psalm, 'Into your hands, Lord, I commend my spirit' (Ps. 30). It is well to remember too that suffering and prayer bring spiritual maturity, abandonment to the will of God and trust that in the end all will be well. How simple to say, how hard to achieve.

'That is very well for people like you with time on your hands – monks and nuns – I hear you say, but I haven't time. If only you knew what it was to run a home, look after children, care for ageing parents . . . some of us are busy people. We have things to do.' 'All right, all right, Martha. Be patient. I was coming to the point of this meditation: busy people and prayer.'

Let me speak now about Martha. Martha seemed to be fed up that she had been left to do all the work while Mary just sat around doing little or nothing to help. Martha was quite worked up: 'Lord, do you not care that my sister has left me to serve alone?' she grumbled. She was then told: 'Martha, you are anxious and troubled about many things; one thing is needful . . .' For Martha, too, prayer was necessary.

Now there could be no questioning by Jesus of the value of what Martha was doing. How could he have done so? First of all, the Book of Genesis had taught that we were 'to till the land and make it fruitful'. Work is a co-operating with God to realise the potential that is latent in his creation. Work is essential for the well-being of every individual. Furthermore, Jesus spent thirty years of his life doing the ordinary things of a boy and man of the Palestine of his day. This is of great significance. It means that God recognises the value of everything that is human, except of course that which is sinful. If the Son of God, who was himself God, could as man hold a broom in his hands or help to clear away the dishes, then sweeping the floor and washing-up are pleasing to God and are a way of serving him. Indeed they are and they can be acts of love. Now I am not just speaking about domestic work. What I have said applies to all work, however complex or sophisticated, provided, of course, that there is no sin. It is a sharing in God's creative activity, and thus precious in his sight.

To sit at the feet of the Lord listening and loving is very important. But sitting at the Lord's feet may not be required of us at any given moment. The will of God may be different for us. God requires of us to serve him in those ways that are made clear to us – the duties of our state in life, the demands of the family, the job to be done at work.

Holiness, to which everyone is called, consists in doing the will of God and in accepting it. For the majority of people they have to become saints in the world in which they live ordinary humdrum lives. This is not a second best. Where I am is where I must become holy. Now in order to ensure the ordinary activities of every day may be more consciously directed to God, then prayer must play a part. When we learn to try to raise minds and hearts to God in prayer then we understand better how to bring God into our daily lives and all its different activities. This means making certain that we never omit on any day just a few minutes, or perhaps just seconds, consciously given to prayer. We should, however, get to the stage where we feel that something important is missing if we reach the end of the day without having spent some part of it, however brief, at prayer. We should have that uneasy feeling when we go to bed having failed to make that promised telephone call to the person waiting for us to do so.

Behind all that lies one vitally important truth. The fulfilment of a human life is not in this world but in another. We are made for God, to be one with Him, and to enjoy for ever that happiness which so easily eludes at the present. We shall die, of course, but it is not the end but a new beginning. We shall rise again. Just as we should be grateful to Martha for her profession of faith in Jesus as the Messiah for so long expected, so we have reason to be thankful to her for eliciting from Jesus a clear and unequivocal statement about our future destiny. Jesus had said: 'Your brother will rise again.' To which Martha had answered, 'I know he will rise again at the resurrection on the last day.' Then came Jesus's teaching:

'I am the resurrection. Anyone who believes in me, even though that person dies, will live, and whoever lives and believes in me will never die.' Then he asked: 'Do you believe this?' Martha made her profession of faith.

Thank you, Martha, for getting Jesus to give us this precious word.

To recognise that life is short, that it does not end with death, that we have a home that is elsewhere – all this brings perspective to today's problems and prevents our living as if there were nothing but life on earth. It took time to recover from that first childhood encounter with death, Frank's death, but slowly over the years an understanding of death developed. Apprehension remains but prayer helps to empty it of its worst terrors.

The three sisters and brother who lived at No. 11 were a welcoming household, generous with time and hospitality. When we knocked at the door, it was opened and we were immediately at home. The hospitality was warm but not lavish. After all we were children and were received in a manner appropriate to our ages. Had the visitor been Christ, it might have been otherwise. For him we would wish to do our best. We would anoint him with our best gifts, sparing no expense.

He knocks at our doors, today and every day, and waits for us to open and admit him into the intimacy of our lives. We have the frightening power to keep the door shut and refuse him entry. And we may wish to do so. There is always within us a part of ourselves which is for us alone. We are not to be disturbed, we do not wish to respond to any demand he may make on us, his presence may prove to be too uncomfortable. And yet he goes on knocking. 'Behold, I stand at the door and knock; if anyone hears my voice and opens the door, I will come to him [and her] and eat with him, and he with me' (Rev. 3:20)

If we open ourselves to him we discover a friend, not for us the awkward and often embarrassing silence of a stranger. But it means admitting him into our minds and into our hearts, spending a few moments, like Mary, at

his feet in order to serve better, as Martha did, wherever
our busy lives may take us.

Yes, he knocks. Let him in.

SEARCHING FOR GOD

Cardinal Basil Hume

'The principles which guide the monk in his search for God and the Gospel values are relevant to both Christians and non-Christians alike,' writes Cardinal Hume. Adapted from addresses he gave while Abbot of Ampleforth, *Searching for God* radiates the joy and humour which characterise his own faith, as he discusses the ever-present problems for anyone attempting to obey the twofold command to love both God and neighbour.

'An exploration into God . . . He is honest until it hurts.'
Times Literary Supplement

TOWARDS A CIVILISATION OF LOVE

Cardinal Basil Hume

'We are called to be physicians of that civilisation about which we dream, the civilisation of love.' Pope John Paul VI

Cardinal Hume brings his pastoral wisdom, his theological expertise, his deep awareness of Church tradition and his personal faith to a fresh examination of the role and potential of the Church today. The vocation and mission of the laity, the fellowship of the people of God, different aspects of ministry, the renewal of spirituality, ecumenism and the local church of the future – all these are considered with sensitivity and clarity of vision. A new chapter on the Christian family takes account of today's trends.

'Warmth, concern and genuineness breathe through every page.'
The Universe

THE IMPACT OF GOD
Soundings from St John of the Cross
Iain Matthew

'This book has been important for me and I think will be important for many others . . . Iain Matthew reveals beautifully the true John of the Cross, firmly centerd in Jesus, in love with Jesus.'
From the foreword by Jean Vanier

John of the Cross testifies to a God who longs to meet us and to love us in our deepest need. Whilst rejection and imprisonment played their part in the life of this 16th-century Spanish friar, John's poetry and prose reveal the beauty and power of a wondrous God. His writing draws us gently along the road of deepening relationship with this God of love, into the immense depth of life-giving prayer. It gives us courage to believe in the possibility of change in our own lives, however unlikely or impossible this may seem.

A JOURNEY INTO GOD

Delia Smith

A Journey into God is a profound reflection on a subject of deep personal significance to Delia Smith: prayer. Written with the same spirit of simplicity and good sense which has characterised her approach to cookery, this book is ideal for personal use or as a gift.

'A spiritual classic for today.'
David Konstant, Bishop of Leeds

'A useful and practical guide.'
The Sunday Times

'Welcome nourishment for a spiritual journey.'
Derek Worlock, Archbishop of Liverpool

'A book for the non-believer and, perhaps even more so, for the not-quite-believer – and this must include an awful lot of us.'
Barry Norman

THE RESTLESS HEART

Ronald Rolheiser

'Loneliness is not a rare and curious phenomenon,' writes Ronald Rolheiser. 'It is at the centre of every person's ordinary experience.' Examining current theories on the causes of loneliness and using modern-day parables from literature, the cinema and his own experience, the author identifies different types of loneliness: some are to be avoided, some endured and others positively entered into. This outstanding book will reassure and free many to live more meaningfully.

FORGOTTEN AMONG THE LILIES

Ronald Rolheiser

In a series of short essays, some of which appeared in *The Catholic Herald*, Ronald Rolheiser comments on our struggle to move 'beyond the obsessions, restlessness, fears and guilts that rob us of the spirit of our own lives, of the feel of our own cold and warmth, of the taste of our own coffee, and of the consolation of God'. The goal of our journey, he writes, is the type of freedom that allows us to love and celebrate life with God and each other.

'Ronald Rolheiser invites us to look beyond the surface of our lives. He gives us permission to be human. He is a gifted communicator and I personally value his writings very much.'
Delia Smith

THE SHATTERED LANTERN

Ronald Rolheiser

In our busy, fragmented world, it becomes increasingly difficult to sense God's presence. Why is this? Can anything be done to recapture the wonder of God's reality in our lives?

In this wide-ranging analysis of the atheism of our age, Ronald Rolheiser identifies clear obstacles to our appreciation of God such as self-preoccupation, the emphasis on the useful and efficient, and the fast pace of life. He shows how the practice of contemplation is vital to the recovery of a purity of heart that naturally brings awareness of God.

'The road back to a lively faith is not a question of finding the right answers, but of living in a certain way, contemplatively. The existence of God, like the air we breathe, need not be proven. It is more a question of developing good lungs to meet it correctly.'

AGAINST AN INFINITE HORIZON

Ronald Rolheiser

The popular columnist of *The Catholic Herald* presents a far-flung overview of our contemporary lives in this companion volume to his award-winning *Forgotten Among the Lilies*. Writing with characteristic compassion and wit, Ronald Rolheiser looks beyond the horizon of our times. In doing so he offers quiet, sane advice on such subjects as marriage, family life and the presence of God, loneliness and sexuality, death and birth, social justice and humility, God's unconditional love, language and prayer.

'I have a friend who swears by Ronald Rolheiser. Unless she is able to read him regularly, she suffers from spiritual malnutrition. Now I understand her feelings.'
David Forrester, The Tablet